NICE GUYS
ONLY FINISH LAST
IF THEY'RE SLOW.
Alex Zanardi not only won this year's PPG CART World Series Championship, he won the hearts of fans with his warmth, humor and commitment to causes like St. Jude Children's Research Hospital.
TARGET

The NASCAR Manufacturer's Champion Ford Thunderbird of Dale Jarrett.

The NHRA Funny Car Champion Ford Mustang of John Force.

The SCCA Trans-Am Champion Ford Mustang of Tommy Kendall.

The SODA Off-Road Champion Ford F-Series of Scott Douglas.

© 1998 B&WT Co
KOOL
KLEIN
KOOL
KOOL
KLEIN TOOLS
KOOL
KOOL
SURGEON GENERAL'S WARNING: Quitting Smoking Now Greatly Reduces Serious Risks to Your Health.

B
KOOL
KOOL
KOOL
SPONSORED BY
KOOL
CIGARETTES
100's, 17 mg. "tar", 1.3 mg. nicotine av. per cigarette by FTC method.

CONTENTS

Headliners of 1997

CART/PPG Cup

Indy Racing League

NASCAR/Winston Cup

Barber Dodge Pro Series

Trans-Am Tour

Professional SportsCar Racing Exxon WSC and GTS

Published by: Autosport International, Inc.
Publisher: John H. Norwood
Associate Publisher: Barbara Hassler-Steig
Design Director: Robert Steig
Editor: Jonathan Hughes
Front Cover Photography: Geoffrey Hewitt, Nigel Kinrade, Bob Steig, Steve Swope
Back Cover Photography: Steve Swope
Contributing Photographers: Cheryl Day Anderson, Dan Bianchi, Michael C. Brown, Richard Dole, Geoffrey Hewitt, Nigel Kinrade, Ron McQueeney/IMS, Phillip Salazar, Shelly Schmidt, Bob Steig, Steve Swope, Sidell Tilghman

Motorsports America, The Men & Machines of American Motorsport, 1997-98
is published by Autosport International, Inc.
37 East 28 Street, Suite 408, New York, NY 10016

Distributed in the U.S. by Motorbooks International, Osceola, WI 54020
Printed in the U.S.A.

"Nothing reveals more about a race car and its driver than a 24-hour road race."

Hurley Haywood

Few race car drivers have stood up to the demands of endurance racing as well as Hurley Haywood. With five wins at the *Rolex 24 at Daytona,* three at Le Mans and two at Sebring, he is the world's leading long-distance driver.

Haywood's success is a testament to his patience and discipline as much as to his skill. "In endurance racing," says Hurley, "you're always trying to stay just within the outer limits of your car. Push it too hard, and you'll never finish. Don't push it hard enough, and you'll never win."

Staying within that zone requires remarkable precision. "A top driver consistently clocks laps within a few tenths of a second," he says. It also requires a rare empathy with the nature and quality of mechanical objects. Hurley Haywood has driven many cars to victory lane, but he has always relied on one special piece of equipment. "I've worn a Rolex for over twenty years," he says, "and it's never let me down."

ROLEX

Rolex Oyster Perpetual Daytona Cosmograph in stainless steel and 18kt gold with matching Oysterlock bracelet.

For the name and location of an Official Rolex Jeweler near you, please call 1-800-36ROLEX.

THE STREAK

MORE CHAMPIONSHIPS.

FIA Formula One *1997 Champion:*
Jacques Villeneuve, Williams/Renault
Goodyear Racing Eagles

World of Outlaws®
1997 Champion:
Sammy Swindell
Goodyear Racing Eagles

NHRA Pro Stock
1997 Champion:
Jim Yates, Pontiac Firebird
Goodyear Racing Eagles

NHRA
Federal Mogul Dragster
1997 Champion:
Rick Santos
Goodyear Racing Eagles

SERIOUS FREEDOM

1997 PROFESSIONAL RACING
FINAL SCOREBOARD

GOODYEAR	615
VISITORS	227

Results based on the professional series in which Goodyear competes.

CONTINUES.

MORE PLACES. MORE OFTEN.

NASCAR
Winston Cup
1997 Champion:
Jeff Gordon,
Chevrolet Monte Carlo
Goodyear Racing Eagles

Professional SportsCar
1997 Champion:
Butch Leitzinger,
Ford/Riley & Scott
Goodyear Racing Eagles

NHRA Top Fuel
1997 Champion:
Gary Scelzi
Goodyear Racing Eagles

NASCAR
Busch Grand National
1997 Champion:
Randy LaJoie,
Chevrolet Monte Carlo
Goodyear Racing Eagles

SCCA Trans Am
1997 Champion:
Tom Kendall,
Ford Mustang
Goodyear Racing Eagles

NHRA Funny Car
1997 Champion:
John Force,
Ford Mustang
Goodyear Racing Eagles

NASCAR
Craftsman Truck Series
1997 Champion:
Jack Sprague,
Chevrolet
Goodyear Racing Eagles

ASA
1997 Champion:
Kevin Cywinski,
Pontiac Grand Prix
Goodyear Racing Eagles

NASCAR
Featherlite Modified
1997 Champion:
Mike Stefanik, Chevrolet
Goodyear Racing Eagles

SCCA
World Challenge T-1
1997 Champion:
Peter Cunningham,
Acura NSX
Goodyear Eagle
Street Radials

NHRA
Federal Mogul Funny Car
1997 Champion:
Frank Manzo,
Dodge Avenger
Goodyear Racing Eagles

NASCAR
REB-CO Northwest
1997 Champion:
Kelly Tanner,
Chevrolet Monte Carlo
Goodyear Racing Eagles

IROC
1997 Champion:
Mark Martin,
Pontiac Firebird
Goodyear Racing Eagles

SCCA
World Challenge T-2
1997 Champion:
Pierre Kleinubing,
Acura Integra
Goodyear Eagle
Street Radials

NASCAR Goody's Dash
1997 Champion:
Mike Swaim, Jr.,
Pontiac Sunfire
Goodyear Racing Eagles

NASCAR
Featherlite Southwest
1997 Champion:
Bryan Germone,
Chevrolet Monte Carlo
Goodyear Racing Eagles

IHRA Top Fuel
1997 Champion:
Paul Romine
Goodyear Racing Eagles

Hooters ProCup
1997 Champion:
Mario Gosselin,
Chevrolet Monte Carlo
Goodyear Racing Eagles

GOODYEAR
#1 in Racing. #1 in Tires.

Nigel Kinrade

Two for the title... Hendrick Motorsports Driver Jeff Gordon and Crew Chief Ray Evernham... NASCAR's Best

Dan Bianchi

Two for the title... Target/Ganassi Engineer Mo Nunn and Driver Alex Zanardi ...CART's Best

ZANARDI ZOOMS TO THE TOP
for Target/Ganassi's Second Championship in a Row

By Lewis Franck

In top level motor racing there's a fine line between flat out driving and over aggressiveness. After winning his first CART PPG Cup championship before the last race of the year, the new titleholder elaborated on his view of the difference.

The 1996 CART Rookie of the Year walked that fine line with great success in 1997 taking five wins and four poles, despite taking himself out of the season ending Marlboro 500 at California Speedway with a bit of over enthusiasm that resulted in a practice crash.

Zanardi's view, "I'd rather try to tell you why I am winning, even if I occasionally have to justify some moves... rather than offer you reasons for not winning."

One of his racing trademarks is a never quit attitude, even after falling to the back of the pack. At Cleveland, he was hit with a penalty for running over his teammate's airhose, and another for ignoring a CART pit signal. All this after qualifying on the pole.

Commenting on that race, the 31 year old noted, "When I fell down to 22nd after the two penalties I had to pay, I was a bit depressed. I felt the race was gone. I did a couple of laps, maybe overdriving. Overdriving, and I still couldn't get in front of cars that were a couple of seconds slower than mine. At that point, I just decided that I was not going to let my anger run my driving. I decided that I was going to do my best no matter where I ended up that day. I said to myself, 'Look, you have to drive and forget about the race. Just try to get the best out of this car. Drive it like you do in qualifying.' But you have to do that for 70 laps," he pointed out, in traffic to boot.

It worked. Winning that race, his second of five wins, put his title hopes into high gear. Two races later, the ex-Formula One driver underscored his salutary season with a win at the U.S. 500 on the demanding high banks of Michigan International Speedway. This win put him at the top of the points standings. There he remained, for the balance of the season. Not bad for a driver who hadn't seen an ultra high-speed oval, or any oval, until 1996.

There were some low points along his way to the PPG Cup. He was stung by criticism for taking the line from Bryan Herta, at the Molson Indy Vancouver, causing Herta to end up in the wall. This, of course, was the same Bryan Herta who was the victim of Zanardi's "off road" pass at Laguna Seca in 1996.

"In this business you are required to make decisions under pressure. On occasion, the time you have to decide is like the blink of an eye." he said. After watching a replay of the race, Zanardi stated that what he did was the only thing he could do.

Zanardi noted that his performance was due in large part to the diligence and dedication of his crew on the Target/Ganassi team. He singled out his warm relationship with engineer, Morris "Mo" Nunn, the acknowledged reigning genius among racing aerodynamicists.

"Most people don't know that I had to work very hard just to get to meet Chip Ganassi. Just to get the possibility of testing one of his cars. People see things when they are all done."

"When you show up for the first race, they don't see all the winter tests, they don't see all the preparation, they don't see all the effort put in."

"When it finally happens, when you finally win races, when you finally achieve consistency, this is what counts; not just one race, because you can win one race if you are lucky. If you finally do that, it means that there is a lot you've been able to put in..." he said emphatically.

Zanardi affectionately went back to his relationship with Mo Nunn, like himself, a Formula One veteran. "I got on very well with Mo, very well because he reminds me a lot of my old man. Unfortunately, I lost my father three years ago and I miss him a lot. Maybe there is something there I can't explain. On top of everything, Morris gives me answers to my questions that are accurate," said Zanardi. "He says that 'I'm Italian and I'm too hot.' I think he's too cold because he's always very conservative."

"I think that we meet in exactly the right point. I push him very, very hard and I make him do things he would never do by himself, maybe too scared to try. And he slows me down enough because otherwise I would try everything. We really balance each other very well."

Putting all the pieces together, they have found a recipe for success. "Getting in the car and squeezing the throttle is five percent; it's not simply five percent, but it's the last five percent. All the first 95 percent has to be done right. There are a lot of drivers capable of squeezing that throttle well. They may do that five percent job right, but if they squeeze the throttle and everything else has not been set the way it should, that guy can end up not looking so good."

Zanardi doesn't have too much time to savor his title. Mo Nunn announced his retirement from the team and motor racing at the end of the season. For all his talent at the wheel, driving without Mo will be a lot tougher for Zanardi.

Cheryl Day Anderson

Close Competition... All eight 1997 Marlboro Pole Award winners, the most in any single season are seated prior to the California 500, from left, Alex Zanardi, Mauricio Gugelmin, Bryan Herta, Scott Pruett, Paul Tracy, Gil de Ferran, Raul Boesel, and Dario Franchitti. Zanardi collected four poles and the Cleveland win from the pole for $130,000. Tracy's two poles and Nazareth win from the pole earned him $80,000. Gugelmin's three poles were worth $30,000. De Ferran, Pruett, and Herta scored two each. Rookie Dario Franchitti notched one. Tracy remains the all-time money winner with $365,000 over the award's five year history. He's shown with Marlboro's Ina Broeman.

Marlboro
RESET
METER
3

16 mg "tar," 1.1 mg nicotine av. per cigarette by FTC method.
D4
SURGEON GENERAL'S WARNING: Cigarette Smoke Contains Carbon Monoxide.
Marlboro
TEAM PENSKE
Marlboro
SPONSORED BY
Marlboro
CIGARETTES

This is our
Lambeau Field.
Our Boston Garden.
Our Camden Yard.
We play
on asphalt
and concrete.
Grass is for
the infield.
No matter
the sport,
we're all
athletes.
But out here,
when things get rough,
you can't call a time-out.
TOYOTA motorsports
PPG/CART World Series racing. Where athletes move at speeds up to 240 mph. Witness the Toyota-powered MCI and Castrol/Jockey cars and you'll soon understand why Indy car racing is one of the fastest sports in the world. Toyota Motorsports. Our minds are always racing.
www.toyota.com
©1997 Toyota Motor Sales, U.S.A., Inc.

Jeff Gordon, Puts His Stamp on the NASCAR Scene

By Benny Phillips

For Jeff Gordon, the 1997 Winston Cup season ended like the day after a wedding party, smelling sweetly of last night's champagne.

Gordon came to the final round at the newly designed Atlanta Speedway with a 77 point lead over Dale Jarrett, an 87 point advantage over Mark Martin and a slight sense of unease. A practice accident on a slippery pit row cost him his primary car, and left him in an unfamiliar 37th place starting position. In the race he ran conservatively but well enough to beat Jarrett by 14 points and Martin by 29, securing his second championship in three years. It was the third straight title won by Hendrick Motorsports: two by Gordon's team (in 1997 and 1995) and one by Terry Labonte's team (in 1996).

Gordon, 26, became the youngest two-time champion in NASCAR history. He drove his Chevrolet to 10 victories during the season, earning more than $6 million. Among his laurels was the Winston Million. Gordon was only the second driver in history to accomplish that feat. His trips to victory circle included wins in the Daytona 500, the Coca-Cola 600 at Charlotte and the Southern 500 at Darlington to earn R.J. Reynolds' big bonus. Only Bill Elliott had captured it previously.

Gordon's success was in stark contrast to the off track woes of team owner Rick Hendrick, who was battling leukemia and a federal indictment which ended in a plea bargain.

Gordon, himself, breezed through the season in style, a contender on the track as he moved smoothly from one race to another, and, with the media, as he shuttled from one interview to another on the track and off, Gordon handled his assignments with the ease of a busboy putting rolls on a table. Repeatedly, he gazed into a bank of bright lights. He blinked at the TV cameras as if he were an accountant for the Internal Revenue Service on coffee break from a dark office where he added up long columns of figures from dawn til dusk. He always wore the sunglasses which he's paid to wear when he gets out of his race car in victory lane.

He smiled, listened attentively and considered every question thoughtfully as interrogators repetitiously probed to find the how and why behind the things he does.

"We have a great team," he said at least 500 times over the season. "The track came to us late in the race, and on the last stop we hit a super set of tires. That's just racin'."

Sure, it's *just racin'* the way Michelangelo was *just paintin'* and Shakespeare was *just scribblin'*.

Gordon has touched his brush to the canvas in victory circle 29 times in only five full seasons of Winston Cup competition.

The pickers of nit who would look for cracks in the ceiling of the Sistine Chapel downgrade Gordon's year by pointing out that Dale Earnhardt did not have a good season, nor did Terry Labonte or three or four more who are usually in the thick of the points race.

But that is just it, and, boo him or not, to find fault with Gordon, you can only compare him with Gordon. He also won 10 races in 1996 while Labonte won just two and was winning the championship, Gordon won the title the year before. This guy Gordon is the closest thing in racing to being automatic, and that is saying something in a sport that is becoming highly saturated.

"All I'm thinking about out there is winning," he said 100 times. Based on the record, it must be true.

It is attention to detail by his entire team - as if working on the bomb squad - that helps carry Gordon.

Gordon does more than simply drive fast. He does what Joe Montana did with a football and what Michael Jordan does with a basketball. He sees angles and openings and all sorts of possibilities that nobody else sees, and he dances to music that nobody else can hear. Like Montana and Jordan, he takes the game to a level beyond his physical talents.

Jarrett and Martin were the only two drivers who seriously challenged Gordon for most of the season. Martin was close in early fall, but his crewmen, except for one, found out in September at Martinsville they would not be back with Martin in 1998. Martin and team owner Jack Roush made it clear that Martin and one crewman would move from Liberty, NC to a new shop in Charlotte. Martin's crew in Liberty felt cast out to sea on a boat named "Unwanted." They carried out responsibilities the rest of 1997, but in their spare time were not seen hawking Martin souvenirs.

Jarrett rallied for a strong finish. When he was hot, he was hot, but the Robert Yates Ford team lacked the consistency of Gordon's operation.

There were no others to seriously challenge Gordon. Jeff Burton's bid to make a name for himself started too late in the season. Earnhardt was consistent, despite his unexplained solo wall banging episode at Darlington, but his car was not. 1996 champion Terry Labonte never got it off the ground. Late in the season, Labonte's team lost Gary DeHart, its crew chief, who lost his temper at Martinsville and punched out a member of the Hendrick organization. While others had problems, Gordon was on cruise control. It turned out to be the most important season of his career. It led to NASCAR's hottest prodigy signing with the William Morris talent agency, joining such

Nigel Kinrade

California Speedway's Les Richter surrounded by the drivers vying for top honors in the California 500

clients as former president Gerald Ford, Bill Cosby and Clint Eastwood.

This could possibly mean that Gordon would turn up in all sorts of venues, from movies to TV sitcoms. He is the only stock car driver the Morris agency has represented.

While NASCAR is celebrating its 50th anniversary this season, its driver of the moment and, by indications, the future, is a good choice to deliver the broader audience stock car racing wants so badly. Gordon is not exactly a stranger now.

Through 1997, in only five seasons, he won 29 races, claimed two Winston Cup titles and hauled in more than $16 million in winnings. Last year, he earned $6.5 million in endorsements, according to *Forbes* magazine.

Currently, signing Gordon as a spokesperson is a seven figure proposition. He has endorsed his share of automotive staples, modeled a milk mustache on billboards nationwide and passed the time with Shaquille O'Neal and Deion Sanders in a Pepsi TV commercial. He did a solo Pepsi commercial during the Super Bowl in which his race car zoomed up a wall and over other cars as Gordon, in the driver's seat, fumbled for a Pepsi can. Crew chief Ray Evernham explained, "We gotta get him a cup holder."

"I never knew there was this side of racing," Gordon, who began playing with automobiles at age 5, said. "When I was younger, I was the shyest kid on the block, so getting in front of a TV camera was the last thing I wanted to do. Now, I enjoy working with sponsors. I enjoy working on new projects and seeing the creativity of a commerial, a promotion, or advertising in general."

Gordon's racing ability took a step forward in 1997. He won races on superspeedways, intermediate ovals and short tracks, while also posting the first road course victory of his career at Watkins Glen in August. Gordon won, in order of the schedule, at Daytona, Rockingham, Bristol, Martinsville, Charlotte, Pocono, California, Watkins Glen, Darlington and New Hampshire. He did not win in the last seven races of the season.

In fact, Gordon had to overcome adversity at Atlanta in the season finale. His 77 point lead over Jarrett and 87 point margin over Martin seemed safe enough. Then problems began at the start of the second practice session on Saturday. Friday was lost to rain.

Gordon was going down pit road and ran into the rear of Bobby Hamilton's Pontiac, parked and waiting. Both teams (Richard Petty owns Hamilton's car) involved had to go to secondary cars.

Then, on his qualifying lap, Gordon slipped in the first turn, nearly losing control. It cost him probably half a second, and he ended up 37th in the starting field. Jarrett started third and Martin ninth. Gordon had to finish the race 18th or better, and it would not matter where Jarrett or Martin finished. Geoff Bodine won the pole at 197.478 mph in a Ford, the fastest qualifying run since Bill Elliott at Talladega in 1990 when he toured the 2.66 mile track at 199.388 mph.

if this is your life, this is your network.
The leader in motorsports coverage.SM
TNN MOTOR SPORTS SM
Visit our Web site www.country.com
© 1998 CBS Cable. All rights reserved.

The new design at Atlanta and resurfacing of the track led speeds well above what competitors considered safe. Bodine talked about winning the pole. "You take a deep breath and go for it," he said. "The one lap run is mind boggling and breathtaking, so I don't know what 500 miles is going to be like."

The mystery unfolded on a cold November afternoon. Bobby Labonte drove his Pontiac to victory in the finale as he did the year before. He dominated, leading 168 of 325 laps.

Gordon shepherded his points lead and won the championship. He struggled to a 17th place finish and won the title by 14 points over Jarrett. Martin finished third in the race and third in the standings, 29 points behind Gordon and 15 back of Jarrett.

Gordon drove a conservative race. He never led a lap and was never close to the front, but he never gave up the points lead.

"Bobby had the best car," Martin said. "We gave it our best shot, but broke something in the engine. At least we finished third. That's all we had and it wasn't going to win the championship anyway.

Dale Jarrett said his car was not exactly right, "I think I had a carburetor problem all day," he said.

Gordon did what he had to do. He tip-toed through traffic and stayed out of trouble. He stroked as winners before him have when they come to Atlanta with a comfortable points lead. It will happen again in the future.

"It certainly was not the best weekend for us," Gordon said, "but it was an unbelievable day. This wasn't the way I wanted to do it, but we pulled it off and that is what counts. We didn't do it in style today, but we did it in style all year."

Gordon said he did not sleep well Saturday night, and worried before the race. In fact, he said he had not slept well in two weeks. "Then we took off, and the car felt good. That made me feel better, but all of a sudden some guys started pulling away. It was as if they adjusted their cars. We couldn't keep up, so I started worrying again."

Gordon talked about hitting Hamilton in Richard Petty's car on Saturday. "That upset me," he said. "I would not have hit anything if the car had not been sitting there. But I would not have hit him if I had not been a bonehead. Pit road was slick and the tires new, but it was totally unnecessary. I was upset with myself."

The champ said he knew he had to put Saturday aside and decide what to do to win the title. "I knew we had to avoid mistakes and race rather hard. Max Helton (minister) got Dale Jarrett, Mark Martin and me, and we all sat down and held hands and had a prayer Saturday night. That was cool. It was classy. It said something for the sport."

Gordon said the track changed with about 100 miles to go. "I was running at a comfortable pace. The car was not capable of running up front, but it was capable of running about 12th or 13th. All of a sudden, I had to run hard on one set of tires. It seemed as if I abused the right rear, and the car started getting away from me going into the corners. I had to back off and lost some positions. I told Ray Evernham, my crew chief, I felt that if we didn't pit early, we might lose more positions. So, we came in early and pitted. That meant I had to run the last 50 or so miles on a set of tires. I tried to pace myself and save the tires. It worked out fine."

Evernham said the team did not get conservative until Sunday morning. "We came to Atlanta with every intention of winning this race, but we expected to do it with the other car, the one we wrecked. Then we made the mistake on pit road. After that, we overfilled the oil tank on the back up car. Oil came out on the rear wheels, and we didn't get a good qualifying spot. It rained Saturday afternoon and canceled Happy Hour. We came out to the track Sunday morning and said we need to be 15th."

"I promise someday we are going to win one of these things in Earnhardt style. We put a lot of work into this season. The most important thing all year long was to win this championship, so we didn't want to go out and do something stupid in the last race."

Gordon and Evernham had earned the right to stroke. To win not only 10 races but to win the Daytona 500, the Winston Million, the road course and everything else, they could be excused for one day of slow-poking around.

Jarrett won seven races during the year and Martin four. While Gordon, Jarrett and Martin were the talk of the town, other drivers shared main street at times in 1997. Jeff Burton earned his first victory in the inaugural race at Texas Motor Speedway. He would win twice more before the end of the season to bring his Jack Roush-owned Ford home fourth in the points.

Dale Earnhardt did not win a race for the first time in 15 years. He finished fifth in the points standings but Earnhardt made headlines at Darlington in September when he passed out during the first few laps of the Southern 500. After successfully undergoing a battery of medical tests, he was back on the track the following week.

Little John Andretti won at Daytona in July to earn his first Winston Cup victory and the first for Cale Yarborough as team owner.

Ricky Rudd won the third race of the season and the big one at the Brickyard. Bill Elliott was winless. Defending champion Terry Labonte did not win until October and finished sixth in the points. Ernie Irvan and Bobby Hamilton were the only other drivers to post victories during the campaign.

While others did well, 1997 belonged to Gordon. He says he is living a dream. "I didn't honestly believe I was going to have the success I've had," he said after the season ended. "Now I am living that dream and saying even I never thought it would come true. It is a great feeling, but I don't think I can really know what it all means until somewhere down the road when I can look back. I think when you're living it, you're so focused on what's going on at the moment and what the next step is that you don't really enjoy it as much as you can when your career is over."

That's just racin'.

Like the busboy, Jeff Gordon cleared the table for another party.

Nigel Kinrade

1 Back on Top... **Jeff Gordon**, the '96 runner-up, regained the top rung of the Winston Cup ladder he first occupied in '95. Once again the top race winner with 10, including the season opening Daytona 500. The Chevrolet driver's performance was virtuoso level, except for a miscue in the season ending NAPA 500 at Atlanta. Won the Winston Million, helping make him NASCAR's biggest single season earner at $6.37 million. He scored a single Busch pole. (4710 Winston Cup points)

Nigel Kinrade

2 Persistent Pursuer... Dale Jarrett gained the Winston Cup lead in March, lost it in May. Came back strong with five second half victories to put pressure on points leader Gordon right up to the final event. The top Ford driver compiled seven victories, the year's second highest total, notched three Busch poles. (4696 Winston Cup points)

Nigel Kinrade

3 Ford Flyer... Mark Martin led the Winston Cup parade after the Bristol round in August, battled mightily with Gordon and Jarrett down the stretch, was in the running til the end. His four victories were the third highest total of the year, and his winning average at Talladega was NASCAR's fastest ever. Three Busch poles tied him for the year's qualifying leadership. (4681 Winston Cup points)

Nigel Kinrade

4 Three Time Winner... Jeff Burton posted the victory at the Texas Motor Speedway inaugural, plus two others, for the year's fourth highest win total, three. It was a banner year for the Ford driver, only two seasons out of the rookie ranks. (4285 Winston Cup points)

Nigel Kinrade

5 Consistency Counts... Dale Earnhardt one of NASCAR's all-time superstars, went winless in '97, still landed in the top five. His strong second place at Talladega after a horrendous crash in '96, was a monument to his courage. (4216 Winston Cup points)

Nigel Kinradee

6 Off the Pace... Terry Labonte, the '96 Winston Cup champion, led the '97 points chase for the month of May, faded in the second half of the tour, managed to notch a single victory. (4177 Winston Cup points)

Nigel Kinrade

7 Loves Atlanta... **Bobby Labonte** returned to the scene of his single '96 triumph, Atlanta, repeated the procedure. He also tied Jarrett and Martin as the top Busch pole producer with three. (4101 Winston Cup points)

Nigel Kinrade

8 Perennially Popular... **Bill Elliott**, beloved by the fans, took down a single Busch pole, 14 top 10 finishes but no wins, to secure a top 10 slot in the season's standings. It was a big move up from a lackluster '96 season. (3836 Winston Cup points)

Nigel Kinrade

9 Richmond Runner... **Rusty Wallace** scored his single victory in the Pontiac Excitement 400 at Richmond International Raceway's 3/4 mile oval. He was often in the lead pack on the demanding short tracks and posted a single Busch pole position. (3598 Winston Cup points)

Nigel Kinrade

10 Back in the Top Ten... Ken Schrader nailed down a spot in the elite top 10 on the basis of two Busch pole positions and eight top 10 finishes, although a victory eluded him. (3576 Winston Cup points)

Nigel Kinrade

11 Just Missed the Top 10... **Johnny Benson**, with eight top 10 finishes, was kept out of the year's top 10 by a single point. (3575 Winston Cup points)

Nigel Kinrade

12 Moving Up... Ted Musgrave's five top five finishes highlighted his year, which moved him up four places over his '96 finish. (3556 Winston Cup points)

Nigel Kinrade

13 New to the Top 20... Jeremy Mayfield's three top five finishes landed him in the year's top 20. (3547 Winston Cup points)

Dan Bianchi

14 Out of the Top 10... Ernie Irvan's two Busch poles and a single race victory weren't enough to keep him in the elite top 10 club. (3534 Winston Cup points)

Nigel Kinrade

15 Back in the Top 20... Kyle Petty had nine top 10 finishes which helped restore him to top 20 status. (3455 Winston Cup points)

Nigel Kinrade

16 Race Winner Again... Bobby Hamilton again scored a win for the Richard Petty team, but dropped out of the year's top 10 (3450 Winston Cup points)

Nigel Kinrade

17 Winning Streak Intact... **Ricky Rudd** kept his 14 year span of at least one victory per year intact, still failed to maintain his top 10 status for the year. (3330 Winston Cup points)

Nigel Kinrade

18 Back Again in the Top 20... **Michael Waltrip**'s six finishes in the top 10 retained his slot in the year's top 20. (3173 Winston Cup points)

Nigel Kinrade

19 More Expected... Ricky Craven maintained his top 20 status but failed to demonstrate his capability as a consistent front runner. (3108 Winston Cup points)

Nigel Kinrade

20 Fast Qualifier... Jimmy Spencer had four top 10 outings, won a single Busch pole, reaffirmed his place in the year's top 20. (3079 Winston Cup points)

Nigel Kinrade

NASCAR Winston Cup Race 1
Daytona 500
Daytona International Speedway
Daytona Beach, FL
February 16, 1997
200 Laps, 500 Miles

JEFF GORDON, TERRY LABONTE AND RICKY CRAVEN FINISH 1,2,3 IN THE DAYTONA 500

IT'S A SWEEP FOR HENDRICK MOTORSPORTS

In a feat unprecedented in NASCAR annals, the three car Hendrick Motorsports team captured the three top places in the Daytona 500. Not that it was easy. Both Gordon and Labonte found themselves at the back of the field through mishaps. Craven was forced to start there when he crashed his primary car in a 125 mile qualifying race. At the start, surprise polesitter rookie Mike Skinner deferred to team member Dale Eanrhardt who led 48 of the first 50 laps, and seemed again a strong candidate to win the big race that has eluded him so long. His frustration continued, as the result of a heartstopping crash on the back straight triggered by Gordon's passing maneuver for second place. Once in second place, with his teammates pushing from behind, Gordon inevitably ran down leader Bill Elliott's Ford with five laps to go. Labonte and Craven followed in their Chevrolets. A downcast Elliott, Ford-mounted, in his best performance in years, finished fourth, was denied the victory by an overwhelming team effort, demonstrating the power of the multiple car draft on superspeedways. The top five drivers following the Daytona 500 were: Jeff Gordon, 180; Terry Labonte, 170; Ricky Craven, 165; Bill Elliott, 165; and Sterling Marlin, 160 points.

Nigel Kinrade

NASCAR Winston Cup Race 2
Goodwrench Service 400
North Carolina Motor Speedway
Rockingham, NC
February 23, 1997
393 Laps, 400 Miles

JEFF GORDON ROLLS AT ROCKINGHAM FOR TWO OUT OF TWO IN '97

The Winston Cup season is still young, but Jeff Gordon has already put his imprint on it, winning the second race of the tour for a perfect record in '97. His primary victim was third fastest qualifier Dale Jarrett, who led 323 of the race's 393 laps. Gordon, who qualified fourth, didn't get in front until lap 351 but was never headed on his way to a 2.692 second margin of victory. Jeff Burton came up front from a 17th place starting slot to finish third. Polesitter Mark Martin ended up a lap down. The race was a classic example of driver/crew chief coordination with Hendrick Motorsports' Ray Evernham marginally improving Gordon's Chevrolet on successive pit stops. Gordon's new teammate Ricky Craven finished fifth, just behind Ricky Rudd, to hold down second place in the Winston Cup points standings. The top five drivers following the Goodwrench Service 400 were: Jeff Gordon, 360; Ricky Craven, 320; Terry Labonte, 316; Jeff Burton, 300; and Ricky Rudd, 298.

NASCAR Winston Cup Race 3
Pontiac Excitement 400
Richmond International Raceway
Richmond, VA
March 2, 1997
400 Laps, 300 Miles

RUSTY WALLACE WINS A CLOSE CONTEST AT RICHMOND

Rusty Wallace, in the Miller Lite Ford, had a busy day on Richmond's .75 mile oval, besting Geoff Bodine and Dale Jarrett by .451 of a second. His Penske Motorsports crew had an even busier day off the track, surviving a stiff post-race inspection and a follow up inspection under laboratory conditions. At the track, Wallace's engine first passed, then failed a test for the maximum 14 to 1 compression ratio allowed. The follow up test cleared the driver and crew; a happy outcome for Wallace and company. NASCAR's penalty for this kind of violation is severe. Fourth place Jeff Gordon, in the DuPont Refinishes Chevrolet, maintained his stance atop the Winston Cup points standings, with teammate Terry Labonte, in the Kellogg's Corn Flakes Chevrolet, seventh today, ensconced in second place. The top five drivers following the Pontiac Excitement 400 were: Jeff Gordon, 525; Terry Labonte, 462; Dale Jarrett, 449; Ricky Rudd, 448; and Ricky Craven, 441 points.

NASCAR Winston Cup Race 4
PrimeStar 500
Atlanta Motor Speedway
Atlanta, GA
March 9, 1997
328 Laps, 500 Miles

DALE JARRETT ON TOP IN ATLANTA'S LAST RACE AS AN OVAL

Dale Earnhardt hated to see Atlanta's true oval configuration go. Small wonder, he had won eight races here. Today, the nod went to another Dale, Dale Jarrett, driving a Ford, who led 253 laps of the 328 contested, including the last 58. Earnhardt failed to get in front for a single tour, but he did drive the first Chevrolet to finish (seventh place). Jeff Gordon, winner of the year's first two races, took a dive in the Winston Cup standings, finishing dead last. Ford-mounted Ernie Irvan posted a strong second place ahead of Pontiac chauffeur Morgan Shepherd. The surprise pole winner and new record setter was Robby Gordon, better known for his exploits as an Indy car driver. He finished a lap down. Jarrett's winning margin was a comfortable 1.38 seconds. The top five drivers following the PrimeStar 500 were: Dale Jarrett, 634; Terry Labonte, 605; Mark Martin, 564; Jeff Gordon, 562; and Bobby Labonte, 533 points.

Nigel Kinrade

NASCAR Winston Cup Race 5
Transouth Financial 400
Darlington Raceway
Darlington, SC
March 23, 1997
293 Laps, 400 Miles

DALE JARRETT DOMINATES DARLINGTON FROM THE POLE

Dale Jarrett was clearly the class of the field in Darlington's Transouth 400, taking the pole, leading the first 28 laps and the last 128 circuits. It wasn't as easy as the statistics would imply. For the last 53 laps, a determined Ted Musgrave tried every device short of banging Jarrett into the wall to get by. None of them worked. Jarrett was ahead by a slim .169 of second at the checker. Musgrave, a bridesmaid on two other occasions in his seven years on the Winston Cup circuit, prefers not to win in predatory fashion. Jeff Gordon, who led briefly on two occasions, finished third, the first Chevrolet driver across the finish line. Winston Cup points leader Jarrett now has nearly a 90 point cushion on Gordon in the new season's standings. The top five drivers following the Transouth Financial 400 were: Dale Jarrett, 819; Jeff Gordon, 732; Terry Labonte, 729; Bobby Labonte, 688; and Jeff Burton, 657 points.

Nigel Kinrade

NASCAR Winston Cup Race 6
Interstate Batteries 500
Texas Motor Speedway
Fort Worth, TX
April 6, 1997
334 Laps, 500 Miles

JEFF BURTON ON TOP IN TEXAS MOTOR SPEEDWAY INAUGURAL

Jeff Burton's first Winston Cup win was a big one, the inaugural event on Bruton Smith's new $100 million Texas Motor Speedway. It earned him $354,350 of a substantial $3.8 million purse. Runner-up Dale Jarrett got $232,800 for his effort which fell 4.067 seconds short, while Bobby Labonte, the third finisher, had to make do with $174,500. Excluded from the handsome payday up front was Jeff Gordon who led twice and was in a contending third place when punted by Ernie Irvan in the aftermath of a Rusty Wallace crash. With qualifying rained out, starting positions were allocated to the top 35 in order of their Winston Cup points standings which put Jarrett on the pole and Gordon alongside him. Terry Labonte finished fourth behind brother Bobby, a reversal of their starting order. The top five drivers following the Interstate Batteries 500 were: Dale Jarrett, 994; Terry Labonte, 899; Bobby Labonte, 858; Jeff Burton, 837; and Jeff Gordon, 810.

NASCAR Winston Cup Race 7
Food City 500
Bristol Motor Speedway
Bristol, TN
April 13, 1997
500 Laps, 266.5 Miles

JEFF GORDON BESTS RUSTY WALLACE ON LAST LAP AT BRISTOL

Jeff Gordon's third win of the new season came at the expense of Rusty Wallace in a last lap shoot out on Bristol's tight half mile. On the 500th and final lap, Gordon, in the DuPont Chevrolet, artistically tapped Wallace, the leader for the previous 74 tours, just hard enough to get by, not hard enough to put Wallace's Ford into the wall. Wallace, the pole-sitter, had led for nearly half the race in his four sessions at the front. Hard on the bumpers of the first two finishers was Terry Labonte, Gordon's teammate and the '96 Winston Cup champion. Dale Jarrett continued on top of the Winston Cup leader board with a solid fourth place finish, while Mark Martin came up from his 23rd starting position to round out the top five. As might be expected, the last lap drama had virtually every fan out of his seat. The top five drivers following the Food City 500 were: Dale Jarrett, 1154; Terry Labonte, 1064; Jeff Gordon, 990; Bobby Labonte, 919; and Jeff Burton, 874 points.

NASCAR Winston Cup Race 8
Goody's Headache Powder 500
Martinsville Speedway
Martinsville, VA
April 20, 1997
500 Laps, 263 Miles

JEFF GORDON MAKES IT TWO IN A ROW AT MARTINSVILLE

Eight races into the '97 tour, Jeff Gordon has won half of them in his DuPont Chevrolet; his fourth victory of the year, at Martinsville, much easier than his Bristol squeaker. He led 432 of the 500 scheduled laps, breezed home comfortably ahead of Bobby Hamilton's STP Pontiac. Hamilton and Joe Nemechek were the only others to get into the lead. Mark Martin came from way back to claim third place. So marked was Gordon's superiority that he even survived a full 360 degree spin initiated when Jimmy Spencer tagged him. This spin allowed Hamilton into the lead. Without it Gordon's winning margin of .356 seconds might well have been larger. The top five drivers following the Goody's Headache Powder 500 were: Dale Jarrett, 1269; Terry Labonte, 1224; Jeff Gordon, 1175; Bobby Labonte, 1061; and Mark Martin, 1029 points.

NASCAR Winston Cup Race 9
Save Mart Supermarkets 300
Sears Point Raceway
Sonoma, CA
May 4, 1997
74 Laps, 187 Miles

MARK MARTIN MASTERS SEARS POINT

Conceded to be one of NASCAR's very best road racers, Mark Martin lived up to his billing by winning from the pole on Sears Point's tricky 2.5 mile layout. Martin had been close before in eight previous appearances on the twisty circuit but had always fallen victim to bad luck in the closing stages. Rusty Wallace, the second fastest qualifier, might have made it a contest, but was sidelined with engine problems. Jeff Gordon got into the hunt at the end but was never a serious threat. He ended up second by .563 seconds. Terry Labonte could have been a threat, but worn tires relegated him to a third place finish. Dale Jarrett's fourth place allowed him to retain his top spot on the Winston Cup leader board. The top five drivers following the Save Mart Supermarkets 300 were: Dale Jarrett, 1434; Terry Labonte, 1384; Jeff Gordon, 1345; Mark Martin, 1214; and Bobby Labonte, 1164 points.

Nigel Kinrade

Nigel Kinrade

NASCAR Winston Cup Race 10
Winston 500
Talladega Superspeedway
Talladega, AL
May 10, 1997
188 Laps, 500 Miles

MARK MARTIN TAMES TALLADEGA FOR TWO IN A ROW

Unbelievably, there were no big crashes in Talladega's Winston 500, nor were there any little crashes, not even a single yellow flag for the fastest 500 miles in the track's history, 185.354 mph. At the end, a smiling Valvoline Ford-mounted Mark Martin had his second win of the year, his second in a row. Dale Earnhardt, back in form, qualified third, finished second, indulged in no heroics to get by winner Martin. Bobby Labonte and his Interstate Batteries Pontiac took down the third finishing spot. Surprise polesitter John Andretti, in the RCA Ford, finished fourth ahead of Jeff Gordon, who is closing in on teammate Terry Labonte, in the Kelloggs Corn Flakes Chevrolet, for the Winston Cup points lead. A bad day at the office dropped Dale Jarrett to third place in the points hunt. The top five drivers following the Winston 500 were: Terry Labonte, 1544; Jeff Gordon, 1501; Dale Jarrett, 1492; Mark Martin, 1394; and Bobby Labonte, 1329 points.

NASCAR Winston Cup Race 11
CocaCola 600
Charlotte Motor Speedway
Charlotte, NC
May 25, 1997
400 Laps, 600 Miles

JEFF GORDON CLAIMS THE COCA-COLA 600 AT CHARLOTTE

Not wind nor rain nor a three hour delay could stop Jeff Gordon, in the DuPont Refinishes Chevrolet, on his way to victory in the rich Coca-Cola 600 at Charlotte Motor Speedway. Nor could runner-up Rusty Wallace, in the Miller Lite Ford; passed by Gordon with 16 laps to go. Short of the scheduled 600 miles, but well past the halfway point that marks an official race, the race's 333 laps ran past midnight under lights after a twilight start. Polesitter Gordon earned $224,900 for his winning effort. Wallace had a $108,025 purse to console him for a workmanlike effort from a midfield start. Mark Martin, winner of the two previous races on the schedule, cooled off slightly for a third place finish. Bill Elliott, in the McDonald's Ford, who led briefly, was fourth. Gordon, aided by the rain, survived a nearly disastrous first pit stop that dropped him all the way to the back of the field. In the battle for the Winston Cup the top five drivers following the Coca-Cola 600 were: Terry Labonte, 1691; Jeff Gordon, 1685; Dale Jarrett, 1579; Mark Martin, 1559; and Bobby Labonte, 1484 points.

NASCAR Winston Cup Race 12
Miller 500
Dover Downs Intl. Speedway
Dover, DE
June 1, 1997
500 Laps, 500 Miles

VICTORY AT DOVER KEEPS RICKY RUDD'S WINNING STREAK INTACT

Ricky Rudd has notched at least one Winston Cup victory every year for 15 years, starting in 1983, a remarkable accomplishment. It's all the more remarkable since his latest win, in the Miller 500 at Dover, brought his career total to 18. A little arithmetic shows that there weren't too many years with multiple wins. By all odds, one of the Robert Yates team of Dale Jarrett and Ernie Irvan, who led a combined total of 406 of the 500 laps, should have won. Jarrett's engine quit while he was leading with 37 laps to go. Irvan crashed out of the lead with nine circuits left. All Rudd, who inherited his lead, had to do was hold off second finisher Mark Martin, which he did. Jeff Burton notched third place. Polesitter Bobby Labonte was never a factor after leading the first 29 tours. The top five drivers following the Miller 500 were: Terry Labonte, 1812; Jeff Gordon, 1775; Mark Martin, 1734; Dale Jarrett, 1656; and Jeff Burton, 1602.

NASCAR Winston Cup Race 13
Pocono 500
Pocono Raceway
Pocono, PA
June 8, 1997
200 Laps, 500 Miles

IT'S GORDON AGAIN AT POCONO

Boosting his winning average to nearly .500, Jeff Gordon added the Pocono 500 to his list of 1997 victories, his sixth out of the 13 contested to date. Starting in 11th place, he got his Dupont Refinishes Chevrolet in front for a single lap on the 20th tour. He regained the lead on lap 133 and took over from Ted Musgrave, in the Family Channel-PrimeStar Ford, for the final 15 laps of the 200 scheduled on Pocono's big 2.5 mile oval. The next five finishers were Ford-mounted, Jeff Burton, second fastest qualifier Dale Jarrett, Mark Martin, Jeremy Mayfield and Musgrave. Polesitter Bobby Hamilton, in the STP Pontiac, led the first 19 laps, was an accident victim on lap 129. Third fastest qualifier Ward Burton had a good race going, with multiple tours in front, until his engine surrendered on lap 141. The top five drivers following the Pocono 500 were: Jeff Gordon, 1955; Terry Labonte, 1955; Mark Martin, 1894; Dale Jarrett, 1826; and Jeff Burton, 1772 points.

Nigel Kinrade

Nigel Kinrade

Precision Pit Work... Jeff Gordon's slick Hendrick Motorsports pit crew puts on four new Goodyears in a handful of seconds. For 1998 and beyond, NASCAR selected Goodyear as the exclusive tire supplier for the Winston Cup, Busch, and NASCAR Craftsman Truck series.

Nigel Kinrade

NASCAR Winston Cup Race 14
Miller 400
Michigan Speedway
Brooklyn, MI
June 15, 1997
200 Laps, 400 Miles

ERNIE IRVAN WINS AT MICHIGAN, SCENE OF HIS NEAR FATAL CRASH

Ernie Irvan always wants to win, but nowhere did he want to win as much as at Michigan where a 1994 practice crash nearly took his life. In a scene out of Hollywood, Dr. Erroll Erlandson,the surgeon who saved Irvan's life, was in the stands and shared the emotional victory. Less emotional but happy nonetheless, was second place Bill Elliott, a non-winner since starting his own team. He finished 2.964 seconds behind the victor. The top four finishers drove Fords, Mark Martin and Ted Musgrave occupying the third and fourth finishing positions. Jeff Gordon piloted the top Chevrolet, finishing fifth. Polesitter Dale Jarrett faded slightly to sixth at the end, just ahead of Dale Earnhardt. Irvan was unchallenged for the last 20 laps. The top five drivers following the Miller 400 were: Jeff Gordon, 2110; Mark Martin, 2064; Terry Labonte, 2001; Dale Jarrett, 1976; and Jeff Burton, 1898 points.

NASCAR Winston Cup Race 15
California 500 Presented by NAPA
California Speedway
Fontana, CA
June 22, 1997
250 Laps, 500 Miles

JEFF GORDON CLAIMS THE CALIFORNIA 500 INAUGURAL

Jeff Gordon, in the DuPont Chevrolet, rolled to his seventh victory in the first 15 races of the 1997 Winston Cup campaign in the inaugural California 500, maintaining a near .500 winning average approaching the season's midpoint. Teammate Terry Labonte, the 1997 champion, was a mere 1.074 seconds behind at the finish, in the Kellogg's Chevrolet. The third fastest qualifier, Gordon needed only eight laps to wrest the lead from Wally Dallenbach who bested polesitter Joe Nemechek on lap two. Neither of these two was a factor at the end. Third place Ricky Rudd topped the Ford contingent at the finish, followed by Ted Musgrave and Jimmy Spencer. Dale Earnhardt had an undistinguished outing, starting 14th and finishing 16th. The new California Speedway got rave reviews from racing teams and spectators alike, the latter turning out in force. The top five drivers following the California 500 were: Jeff Gordon, 2295; Mark Martin, 2203; Terrry Labonte, 2176; Dale Jarrett, 2123; and Jeff Burton, 1971 points.

NASCAR Winston Cup Race 16
Pepsi 400
Daytona International Speedway
Daytona Beach, FL
July 5, 1997
160 Laps, 400 Miles

JOHN ANDRETTI FINALLY GETS HIS FIRST WINSTON CUP WIN

It took him 110 Winston Cup starts to notch his first victory in the series but John Andretti, in the RCA Ford, did it in style. The scene was Daytona International Speedway's Pepsi 400. Among the drivers Andretti bested in the final green flag rundown were such titans of the superspeedways as Terry Labonte, the 1996 WInston Cup champion; Sterling Marlin, a winner at Daytona; and second fastest qualifier Dale Earnhardt. They followed him across the finish line in that order. Andretti, a winner in the CART Indy car series, had bounced around from team to team since moving to NASCAR in 1993 but seems to have found a happy home with his present owner, Cale Yarborough. Jeff Gordon finished outside the top 20. The top five drivers following the Pepsi 400 were: Jeff Gordon, 2400; Terry Labonte, 2346; Mark Martin, 2290; Dale Jarrett, 2278; and Jeff Burton, 2113 points.

NASCAR Winston Cup Race 17
Jiffy Lube 300
New Hampshire Intl. Raceway
Loudon, NH
July 13, 1997
300 Laps, 317.4 Miles

JEFF BURTON BREEZES HOME AT NEW HAMPSHIRE

Jeff Burton's second win of 1997 saw him cruising home by a husky 5.392 second margin over a determined Dale Earnhardt, who started way back in 26th place. Ken Schrader, in the Skoal Bandit Chevrolet, showed some of his qualifying speed of old, taking the pole but finishing just outside the top 10. Dale Jarrett led on three occasions, but finished seven laps down. Rusty Wallace's third place finish represented a solid effort. Burton's teammate, Mark Martin finished fifth, just behind Steve Grissom, piled up some useful points in his title quest. For the second race in a row Jeff Gordon finished outside the top 20, lost his points lead. The top five drivers following the Jiffy Lube 300 were: Terry Labonte, 2497; Jeff Gordon, 2494; Mark Martin, 2445; Dale Jarrett, 2332; and Jeff Burton, 2298 points.

Nigel Kinrade

NASCAR Winston Cup Race 18
Pennsylvania 500
Pocono Raceway
Pocono, PA
July 20, 1997
200 Laps, 500 Miles

DALE JARRETT ON TOP AT POCONO

Last time out at Pocono's big 2.5 mile speedway, Dale Jarrett, in the Quality Care/Ford Credit Ford, made it close, finishing third behind Jeff Gordon. This time he made it stick, taking top honors over Gordon by a sizeable 2.948 seconds. Jeff Burton, in the Exide Batteries Ford, the runner-up in the earlier Pocono outing, had to settle for third place this time. "Front Row Joe" Nemechek, in the BellSouth Chevrolet, notched the pole, but couldn't notch a top 20 finishing position. The clue to Jarrett's relatively easy time in his last 20 laps in front seemed to be his crew's decision to change all four tires, even though this move let Burton, who received only two tires, out in front and into the lead. Jarrett had little trouble running Burton down passing him, and virtually no trouble holding him off. Burton also was passed by Gordon in the DuPont Refinishes Chevrolet. Gordon's third place in the race allowed him to regain the Winston Cup points lead, while teammate Terry Labonte was demoted to the third slot in the season's campaign. The top five drivers following the Pennsylvania 500 were: Jeff Gordon, 2669; Mark Martin, 2605; Terry Labonte, 2555; Dale Jarrett, 2517; and Jeff Burton, 2468 points.

Nigel Kinrade

NASCAR Winston Cup Race 19
Brickyard 400
Indianapolis Motor Speedway
Indianapolis, IN
August 3, 1997
160 Laps, 400 Miles

RICKY RUDD ROLLS TO VICTORY IN NASCAR'S RICHEST RACE, THE BRICKYARD 400

"The fastest isn't always first at the end;" is a racing truism that worked like a charm for Ricky Rudd and his Tide Ford in the Brickyard 400, with nearly $5 million in prize money at stake. Ernie Irvan, in the Texaco Havoline Ford, *was* the fastest in qualifying, he ended up 10th after leading the first 39 laps. Joe Nemechek, in the Bell-South Chevrolet, the second fastest qualifier, was even further down in 32nd place at the finish. Rudd and his crew were masterful in a strategy that allowed them one less fuel stop than most of the field. Runner-up Bobby Labonte, in the Interstate Batteries Pontiac, used the same strategy but lacked the momentum to get around leader Rudd on the last restart. His $242,275 purse provided reasonable consolation. Third finisher Dale Jarrett, in the Quality Care/Ford Credit Ford, appeared to have the fastest car in the final stages but had to make a splash-and-go pit stop. Jeff Gordon, in the DuPont Refinishes Chevrolet, fourth at the end, lost his chance for a repeat victory via the pit stop route, too. Winner, Rudd, basking in the glow of victory lane, earned $571,000 for driving just fast enough to win, while conserving fuel. The top five drivers following the Brickyard 400 were: Jeff Gordon, 2834; Mark Martin, 2755; Dale Jarrett, 2687; Terry Labonte, 2603; and Jeff Burton, 2591 points.

Nigel Kinrade

NASCAR Winston Cup Race 20
Bud at the Glen
Watkins Glen International
Watkins Glen, NY
August 10, 1997
90 Laps, 220.5 Miles

JEFF GORDON WINS AT WATKINS GLEN, HIS FIRST VICTORY ON A ROAD COURSE

Winner Jeff Gordon turned back challenges from NASCAR's best road racers - and a platoon of road racers from other series out for a shot at the Winston Cup regulars on Watkins Glen's demanding road course. Although he finished fourth, ex-CART Indy car driver Robby Gordon probably came closest to depriving Jeff of his first road course victory. Robby lined up in the wrong slot on a restart, was slapped with a stop-and-go penalty, which likely cost him the win. Todd Bodine won the pole but succumbed to engine bothers, leaving brother Geoff the top finisher in the clan, in second place at the end. Rusty Wallace was the third place finisher. Mark Martin, considered by many to be NASCAR's top road racer, could only manage fourth place, giving ground to Gordon in their tussle for the Winston Cup. Wally Dallenbach, John Andretti, and Dorsey Schroeder were among the road racing luminaries who were never in serious contention. The top five drivers following the Bud at the Glen were: Jeff Gordon, 3019; Mark Martin, 2910; Dale Jarrett, 2759; Terry Labonte, 2750; and Jeff Burton, 2667 points.

Nigel Kinrade

NASCAR Winston Cup Race 21
DeVilbiss 400
Michigan Speedway
Brooklyn, MI
August 17, 1997
200 Laps, 400 Miles

MARK MARTIN GETS ASSIST FROM JEFF BURTON, WINS AT MICHIGAN

That's what teammates are for. Down two laps due to a cut tire, eventual winner Mark Martin got a free pass from Roush Racing teammate Jeff Burton, in the Exide Batteries Ford, then the leader, to regain one of them, went on to claim the victory. Burton ended up eighth on the basis of poor pit timing, well behind Martin in his Valvoline Ford. Jeff Gordon managed second place in his DuPont Refinishes Chevrolet. Ted Musgrave occupied third place at the end of the contest. Polesitter Johnny Benson, in the Pennzoil Pontiac, stayed in front for only five laps, ended up down a lap. The top five drivers following the DeVilbiss 400 were: Jeff Gordon, 3194; Mark Martin, 3095; Dale Jarrett, 2914; Terry Labonte, 2884; and Jeff Burton, 2814 points.

Nigel Kinrade

NASCAR Winston Cup Race 22
Goody's Headache Powder 500
Bristol Motor Speedway
Bristol, TN
August 23, 1997
500 Laps, 266.5 Miles

DALE JARRETT THE BARON OF BRISTOL

Dale Jarrett emerged on top in a late race duel of Ford drivers at Bristol. Next in line were Mark Martin, Dick Trickle and Jeff Burton, all in Fords. The bad luck blues landed on Chevrolet driver Jeff Gordon, who led a total of 188 laps in the first two thirds of the event. He was tagged on a restart first by Geoff Bodine and then by Jeremy Mayfield, both a lap down. He hit the wall and dropped to 35th place at the finish, losing ground in the Winston Cup race to Jarrett and Martin, the new points leader. Polesitter Kenny Wallace, was outjumped at the start by Jarrett, did not lead a lap and was a crash victim after 277 laps. The top five drivers following the Goody's Headache Powder 500 were: Mark Martin, 3270; Jeff Gordon, 3257; Dale Jarrett, 3099; Terry Labonte, 3030; and Jeff Burton, 2979 points.

NASCAR Winston Cup Race 23
Mountain Dew Southern 500
Darlington Raceway
Darlington, SC
August 31, 1997
367 Laps, 500 Miles

JEFF GORDON RIDES LUCK TO DARLINGTON WIN AND $1 MILLION WINSTON BONUS

Chevrolet driver Jeff Gordon thought he had the Ford forces fended off when he held off Dale Jarrett for the final 71 laps at Darlington. Not so, on the last lap Jeff Burton charged underneath with the momentum to pass. Gordon veered left tagging Burton. Beaten back, Burton recovered enough to veer right and tag Gordon, not enough, however, to knock him off course and deny him victory, his ninth of '97. Bill Elliott, with new found speed, led three times, was the dominant driver for the first two-thirds of the race, but slipped to fourth at the end. Dale Jarrett, who was in contention all day, finished third after the flying Burton. In a bizarre first lap incident, veteran star Dale Earnhardt drove almost head on into the first turn wall, repeated the process in turn two, and in disoriented condition, had difficulty finding his pit. He was hospitalized overnight after initial tests proved inconclusive Gordon regained the points lead. The top five drivers following the Mountain Dew Southern 500 were: Jeff Gordon, 3437; Mark Martin, 3412; Dale Jarrett, 3269; Terry Labonte, 3180; and Jeff Burton, 3154 points.

NASCAR Winston Cup Race 24
Exide NASCAR Select Batteries 400
Richmond International Raceway
Richmond, VA
September 6, 1997
400 Laps, 300 Miles

DALE JARRETT RIDES HIGH AT RICHMOND

Dale Jarrett's fifth win of '97 came at the expense of runner-up Jeff Burton who had three tours in the lead but was unable to get by Jarrett in the final 38 laps. Tenth fastest qualifier Jeff Gordon finished a solid third, adding useful points to his Winston Cup season total. Polesitter Bill Elliott stayed in front for the first 43 laps, was five laps off the pace at the finish. Much of the fans' interest centered on star driver Dale Earnhardt's return to the racing wars after his opening lap crash at Darlington the previous week, a result of seemingly being asleep at the wheel. He started 22nd, finished 15th, said he felt good. No medical explanation for the crash has surfaced despite intensive medical testing. Rookie Kenny Irwin's Winston Cup debut was outstanding. He started second, finished eighth, leading 12 laps in the process. The top five drivers following the Exide 400 were: Jeff Gordon, 3602; Mark Martin, 3505; Dale Jarrett, 3449; Jeff Burton, 3334; and Terry Labonte, 3292 points.

NASCAR Winston Cup Race 25
CMT 300
New Hampshire Intl. Speedway
Loudon, NH
September 14, 1997
300 Laps, 317.4 Miles

JEFF GORDON HOME FIRST AT NEW HAMPSHIRE ON PIT STRATEGY

Jeff Gordon's crew sent him back into the fray on the last pit stop without fresh tires. Ernie Irvan's team opted for new rubber for the final 72 laps. Gordon, in the DuPont Chevrolet, got out first for the lead, and Irvan couldn't get by despite the presumed tire advantage. The result was bitterly disappointing for Irvan, in the Texaco Havoline Ford, who drove brilliantly from a "way back" 40th starting slot. Second fastest qualifier Bobby Hamilton, in the STP Pontiac, nailed down the third slot at the end after leading for two separate earlier stints. Polesitter Ken Schrader, in the Skoal Bandit Chevrolet, finished nine laps down. The victory was Gordon's 10th of the '97 campaign, enhancing his lead in this key category. The top five drivers following the CMT 300 were: Jeff Gordon, 3787; Mark Martin, 3648; Dale Jarrett, 3599; Jeff Burton, 3455; and Terry Labonte, 3332 points.

Nigel Kinrade

Nigel Kinrade

NASCAR Winston Cup Race 26
MBNA 400
Dover Downs Intl. Speedway
Dover, DE
September 21, 1997
400 Laps, 400 Miles

MARK MARTIN TAMES DOVER'S "MONSTER MILE"

Mark Martin won the MBNA 400 at Dover in convincing style. His Valvoline Ford started on the pole, was 10.334 seconds, a substantial margin by Winston Cup standards, ahead of runner-up Dale Earnhardt in the GM Goodwrench Service Plus Chevrolet, at the end. He was also two laps ahead of prime Winston Cup rival Jeff Gordon, today's seventh place finisher, who started second. Kyle Petty had a good outing, bringing his Pontiac home in third place. Dale Jarrett, in third place on the Winston Cup leader board, managed a fifth place finish, just astern of Bobby Labonte, but stayed very much in the running for the title. With the '97 campaign winding down, Gordon maintains a 100 point lead in the WInston Cup standings over Martin and Jarrett, a respectable but uncomfortable margin. Insiders are predicting that the contest could go down to the last event, as it did in '96. The top five drivers following the MBNA 400 were:Jeff Gordon, 3938; Mark Martin, 3833; Dale Jarrett, 3754; Jeff Burton, 3585; and Terry Labonte, 3384 points.

NASCAR Winston Cup Race 27
Hanes 500
Martinsville Speedway
Martinsville, VA
September 28, 1997
500 Laps, 263 Miles

JEFF BURTON SCORES HIS THIRD WIN OF '97 AT MARTINSVILLE

Winner Jeff Burton, in the Exide Batteries Ford, didn't have to beat Rusty Wallace, his principal opponent all afternoon, in a 20 lap countdown to the wire in Martinsville's Hanes 500. Wallace, in the lead at this late stage, took himself and his Miller Lite Ford out of contention by incurring a stop-and-go penalty for jumping the restart, a miscue that dropped him to 15th at the end. A second miscue in a post-race radio show dropped his bank account by the $5,000 NASCAR fined him for "profanity." Dale Earnhardt, on a strong comeback trail, was the runner-up by .778 seconds while Bobby Hamilton, in the STP Pontiac, who led a few laps toward the end, notched third place. Winston Cup points leader Jeff Gordon's fourth place did nothing to hurt his championship run, while 11th place Mark Martin and 12th place Dale Jarrett, in the Quality Care/Ford Credit Ford, lost ground. The top five drivers following the Hanes 500 were: Jeff Gordon, 4103; Mark Martin, 3968; Dale Jarrett, 3881; Jeff Burton, 3765; and Dale Earnhardt, 3543 points.

NASCAR Winston Cup Race 28
UAW-GM Quality 500
Charlotte Speedway
Charlotte, NC
October 5, 1997
334 Laps, 500 Miles

DALE JARRETT GAINS IN THE TITLE CHASE WITH CHARLOTTE WIN

Luck, abetted by hard driving, was on Dale Jarrett's side in his UAW-GM Quality 500 win at Charlotte. It was conspicuously absent for Bobby Labonte, the Pontiac powered runner-up, who dominated the early going. He was thrown off stride by a spin in front of him, and demoted to the back of the pack on the lead lap. Nonetheless, he soldiered back into the lead on lap 232 of the 334 scheduled. His brilliant drive was mitigated by an engine which went off song, giving Jarrett an uncontested upgrading to first place for the final 58 laps. A resurgent Dale Earnhardt led for two short periods, got by Labonte for second place, gave it back after a brush with Sterling Marlin, settled for third. Fourth place Mark Martin edged Jeff Gordon, who incurred a penalty for speeding in pit row and failed to lead a single lap. Polesitter Geoff Bodine led only four laps, was sidelined via the accident route. The top five drivers following the UAW-GM Quality 500 were: Jeff Gordon, 4268; Mark Martin, 4133; Dale Jarrett, 4061; Jeff Burton, 3920; and Dale Earnhardt, 3713 points.

NASCAR Winston Cup Race 29
DieHard 500
Talladega Superspeedway
Talladega, AL
October 12, 1997
188 Laps, 500 Miles

TERRY LABONTE AVOIDS 21 CAR CRASH, TAKES TALLADEGA

A Jeff Gordon-John Andretti tangle initiated a crash scene involving half of the 42 car field. Terry Labonte avoided it entirely, to win; Ford protagonist and second fastest qualifier Andretti survived it to finish third. Another of the fortunate fifty percent to miss the pile up was Bobby Labonte, who nailed down runner-up honors. The leading Winston Cup contenders Gordon, Mark Martin and Dale Jarrett all finished far down on the board. Chevrolet driver Terry owes a vote of thanks to Pontiac-mounted brother Bobby, who, while not a teammate, was his drafting partner when it counted. It counted most with two laps to go, when they passed the then leader Ken Schrader. Polesitter Ernie Irvan notched the fifth finishing position. Dale Earnhardt, who led on six separate occasions, was involved in the big incident, finished in 29th place. He had predicted that something major could happen at the track where he suffered serious injuries in '96. The top five drivers following the DieHard 500 were: Jeff Gordon, 4321; Mark Martin, 4211; Dale Jarrett, 4166; Jeff Burton, 4041; and Terry Labonte, 3796 points.

Nigel kinrade

Nigel Kinrade

NASCAR Winston Cup Race 30
AC Delco 400
North Carolina Motor Speedway
Rockingham, NC
October 27, 1997
393 Laps, 400 Miles

BOBBY HAMILTON ROLLS AT ROCKINGHAM

Bobby Hamilton, the driver who brought Richard Petty his first victory as a car owner last year, will be leaving the team at the end of the season. His victory at Rockingham, over a surging Dale Jarrett, assures that he'll be leaving in style. Presumably his new job at Chevrolet-based Morgan McClure will be a better paying one, with more chance of a superspeedway win. However, Hamilton had great rapport with his Petty crew members and, in some respects, hated to leave. Starting way back in 28th place he first took the lead on lap 86 and ran out the last 15 laps in the lead for a .941 second margin of victory. Ricky Craven had an "up" day in an up and down season, finished third. Fourth place Jeff Gordon piled up useful points. With two sessions in the lead, he felt that he might have done better. The top five drivers following the AC Delco 400 were: Jeff Gordon, 4486; Mark Martin, 4361; Dale Jarrett, 4341; Jeff Burton, 4095; and Terry Labonte, 3947 points.

NASCAR Winston Cup Race 31
Dura Lube 500 Presented by Kmart
Phoenix International Raceway
Phoenix, AZ
November 2, 1997
312 Laps, 312 Miles

DALE JARRETT WINS AT PHOENIX, TAKES WINSTON CUP TITLE CHASE DOWN TO ATLANTA'S SEASON FINALE

Dale Jarrett's convincing win at Phoenix, combined with Jeff Gordon's 17th place finish put additional pressure on the series points leader going into Atlanta's season finale. Gordon's lead was whittled down to 77 points. Jarrett was essentially in command from the time he took the lead on lap 240 til the finish, 72 circuits later. Runner-up Rusty Wallace, the third fastest qualifier, produced a solid effort, running in front of the field twice, but was no match for Jarrett at the end. Bobby Hamilton, the polesitter and the winner here a year ago, finished third; ahead of Ken Schrader and Dale Earnhardt. Mark Martin kept himself in title contention with a sixth place finish, is now 87 points behind Gordon. The big question in the post-race paddock was, "Will Gordon and crew chief Evernham opt for a safer, cautious game plan in the last race or stick to the early season 'go for broke' approach that netted 10 victories?" Following the Dura Lube 500 the top five drivers were: Jeff Gordon, 4598; Dale Jarrett, 4521; Mark Martin, 4511; Jeff Burton, 4224; and Dale Earnhardt, 4096.

NASCAR Winston Cup Race 32
NAPA 500
Atlanta Motor Speedway
Atlanta, GA
November 16, 1997
325 Laps, 500.5 Miles

BOBBY LABONTE REPEATS '96 ATLANTA VICTORY

JEFF GORDON TAKES THE WINSTON CUP IN CAUTIOUS OUTING

The beneficiary of Goodyear tire testing on the fast, slick new Atlanta Motor Speedway, Interstate Batteries Pontiac driver Bobby Labonte first took the lead on lap 107 and for the fourth and final time on lap 315 of the 325 contested. His victory was clear cut, over season long Winston Cup contenders Ford drivers Dale Jarrett and Mark Martin, the second and third place finishers. Fourth place Jeff Green was the day's top Chevrolet driver. Much of the drama was played out far down in the field, where points leader Jeff Gordon, in the DuPont Chevrolet, started 37th, the result of a pit row practice crash that took out his primary car and a disappointing oil-slicked qualifying run in his backup car. Going into the race he needed 18th place to ensure his title, even if closest points pursuer Jarrett won. Jarrett didn't. His best shot netted him runner-up honors, 3.801 seconds in arrears of the flying Labonte. Martin, too, had a theoretical shot at the title. The best he could do at Atlanta was third, and after a solid but cautious run, a relieved Gordon secured a 17th place finish. He was home safe, with his second Winston Cup in two years and the recipient of the full fledged cheers of a packed stadium. Polesitter Geoff Bodine, in the QVC Ford, finished 11 laps down. Jarrett, in the Ford Quality Care/Ford Credit Ford, and Martin, in the Valvoline Ford, spearheaded a surging contingent of Ford drivers who earned the Manufacturer's Championship for the marque. The top ten Winston Cup drivers following the season finale at Atlanta were: Jeff Gordon, 4710; Dale Jarrett, 4696; Mark Martin, 4681; Jeff Burton, 4285; Dale Earnhardt, 4216; Terry Labonte, 4177; Bobby Labonte, 4101; Bill Elliott, 3836; Rusty Wallace, 3598; and Ken Schrader, 3576 points.

Nigel Kinrade

Nigel Kinrade

1997 Winston Cup Champion Jeff Gordon celebrates his victory, his second title in three years.

Nigel Kinrade

Jeff Gordon Has It All... Two Winston Cups on his mantel, the 1995 and '97 editions, plus a near miss in '96, victories in virtually all of NASCAR's big money races, a handsome bank account (over $6 million in prize money in '97 alone, including the Winston Million), a beautiful and supportive wife, and Ray Evernham, arguably the slickest crew chief in the NASCAR kingdom. Perhaps the only thing he lacks, is the respect of a few fans who want to exercise their time honored right to root against the favorite.

Nigel Kinrade

Dale Jarrett, with seven victories and Mark Martin with four led the front running contingent that won the Manufacturer's Championship for Ford. Martin is shown leading Jarrett in the MBNA 400 at Dover, one of his quartet of wins.

DEBUT AT DAYTONA

The Ford Taurus WInston Cup racer will make its competition debut in the 1998 Daytona 500. It's the first four door model to become a full time competitor in NASCAR's history. Dale Jarrett's Ford Quality Care/Ford Credit entry is shown. Rusty Wallace, Bill Elliott, Jeremy Mayfield and others will drive similar cars. Taurus replaces the Thunderbird which went out in style with 17 wins in 1997 and the manufacturer's title.

The 1998 NASCAR F-150 pickup starts its career as NASCAR's official truck at Daytona, too. Features include black 16 inch, 10 spoke wheels, a front air dam, lowered suspension, and a stainless steel exhaust. Beyond its racing duties, the NASCAR F-150 will be available in limited numbers in dealerships this summer.

JACK SPRAGUE SURGES
to NASCAR Craftsman Truck Series Title

Jack Sprague had everything going for him in the series opener at Disney World Speedway;momentum from victories in the last two '96 events, pole position, the lead with one lap to go and a strong Quaker State Chevy at his command. He understandably expected to win. Joe Ruttman, in the LCI Ford, on Sprague's bumper, had different ideas on the outcome. A few well placed nudges from Ruttman put him in front at the checker, and bumped Sprague all the way down to 15th place. Sprague's championship prospects looked downmarket up until the season's halfway mark, as Rich Bickle, in the DieHard Chevrolet, piled up the points, including those from back to back wins at Portland and Indianapolis Raceway Park. Bickle's lead, at times was more than 100 points. Sprague didn't get on top until the July 31 Cummins 200 at IRP. He was never displaced atop the points parade, though Bickle came close in late September with his Martinsville win, and earned the year's runner-up honors. Consistency was the key, with Sprague running out a string of 12 consecutive top 10 finishes in the second half. Sprague's win total of three matched Bickle's but both had to defer to Ruttman with five victories and 1996 series champion Ron Hornaday with seven, including a remarkable three straight.

Ruttman notched third place in the season's standings with Hornaday checking in at fifth place, a victim of five DNFs. In between, in fourth, came Mike Bliss with only a single victory but a high degree of finishing prowess. Rookie Kenny Irwin, in the Raybestos Ford, was a two-time winner (Homestead and Texas) and easily gained the Cintas Rookie of the Year title. He made the year's top 10 on the points ladder and earned a promotion to Winston Cup ranks with the blue chip Robert Yates team for 1998. Another first year driver, Tony Raines gained his first victory, and Dodge's at the I-70 Speedway in Odessa. Veterans Jay Sauter, Rick Carelli, Jimmy Hensley and Chuck Bown occupied places 6, 7, 8, and 9 on the year end ladder. Of this quartet only Sauter managed a single victory. Other winners, all first timers, included Ron Fellows, a Trans-Am star, Bob Keselowski, and Sauter. Randy Tolsma notched a victory.

Sprague's campaign was a lucrative one. His 1997 record single season earnings of $880,835 put him atop the series' career money chart with $1,577,448. As usual, some Winston Cup regulars made "guest appearances," Morgan Shepherd, Joe Nemechek, Ken Schrader, Ernie Irvan, Bobby Hamilton, Kyle Petty, and Mike Skinner among them. Skinner and Irvan had the best results, a pair of top five finishes. IRL driver Eliseo Salazar made a single start. Lady driver Tammy Jo Kirk made the year's top 20 despite starting only 19 of the year's 26 events. 167 different drivers made at least one start, an indication of the series' continuing growth.

As evidence of the growing sophistication of the trucks being raced, new average speed race records were set at all 25 venues contested except for Homestead, Monroe, Bristol, and IRP (admittedly some of the tracks were new, so that a record was automatic). In this category, the winning average speed at Texas was a blistering 131.823 mph, which was topped at California with 137.195 mph. Only Homestead, Nazareth, and Mesa Marin failed to produce record qualifying speeds. California's 173.198 mph record qualifying was topped by Texas' 175.667 mph. Considering that the aerodynamics of trucks are far from ideal these speeds are remarkable indeed.

Nigel Kinrade

1 Consistency Counts... Jack Sprague missed the top 10 only three times all year, chalked up more top fives (16) than any other driver. Add in three victories, and he posted the winning numbers. (3969 NASCAR Craftsman Truck points)

Nigel Kinrade

2 Early Leader... Rich Bickle led the early season points chase by a solid margin, lost consistency in the stretch run. Three wins and 15 top fives still made for a handsome sesaon. (3737 NASCAR Craftsman Truck points)

Nigel Kinrade

3 Close Call... Joe Ruttman missed runner-up honors by only a single point. His five trips to victory lane were the year's second highest total. (3736 NASCAR Craftsman Truck points)

Nigel Kinrade

4 Moving Up... Mike Bliss had only a single win, but his second highest top 10 total earned him a solid fourth place. (3611 NASCAR Craftsman Truck points)

Nigel Kinrade

5 Top Race winner... **Ron Hornaday**, the 1996 champion, notched seven victories, the year's best output. It wasn't enough to overcome five DNFs. (3574 NASCAR Craftsman Truck points)

Nigel Kinrade

6 Regular Front Runner... Jay Sauter capped his season with a single victory and 15 top 10 placements. (3467 NASCAR Craftsman Truck points)

Nigel Kinrade

7 Regular Top 10 Finisher... **Rick Carelli** tied for the third highest top 10 total of the year with 17. (3461 NASCAR Craftsman Truck points)

Nigel Kinrade

8 Status Maintained... Jimmy Hensley matched his 1996 ranking, scored 13 top 10 finishes. (3385 NASCAR Craftsman Truck points)

Phillip Salaar

9 New to the Top 10... Chuck Bown, the surprise runner-up at Phoenix vaulted into the year's elite top 10. (3320 NASCAR Craftsman Truck points)

Nigel Kinrade

10 Cintas Rookie of the Year... Kenny Irwin posted two victories in his freshman year, indicating star potential. (3320 NASCAR Craftsman Truck points)

Nigel Kinrade

NASCAR Craftsman Truck Race 1
Chevy Trucks Challenge
Walt Disney World Speedway
Orlando, FL
January 19, 1997
200 Laps, 200 Miles

JOE RUTTMAN RIDES THE BUMPS TO VICTORY AT DISNEY WORLD

No, the bumps weren't in the track. The bumps were those delivered to polesitter and race dominator Jack Sprague, in the Quaker State Chevrolet, on the last lap of the Chevy Trucks Challenge by LCI Ford driver Joe Ruttman. These taps enabled then second place Ruttman to get around Sprague for the victory. Sprague was demoted all the way down to 15th. Also benefiting from this encounter were Butch Miller in the Walker Evans Ford, and Rich Bickle, in the DieHard Chevrolet, who grabbed second and third respectively. The qualifying speed, 126.859 mph, and the race average, 88.159 mph, set new records. 1996 series champion Ron Hornaday qualified well, finished way back in 30th place.

NASCAR Craftsman Truck Race 2
NAPA 200
Tucson Raceway Park
Tucson, AZ
March 1, 1997
200 Laps, 75 Miles

RON HORNADAY BOUNCES BACK, TAKES TUCSON'S NAPA 200

Driving the NAPA Chevrolet, a resilient Ron Hornaday rebounded from his dismal Disney outing for a clear cut victory in his sponsor's NAPA 200 at Tucson. He led the last 10 laps, had a handsome 1.304 second margin over runner-up Rich Bickle at the end. Jay Sauter garnered third place in the GM Goodwrench Chevrolet. The surprise polesitter, Michael Dokken, in the DANA Corporation Dodge, faded to 13th place at the end. It was an all Dodge front row at the start with Jimmy Hensley alongside Dokken. Hensley, ended up eighth. Hornaday, who drives for Dale and Teresa Earnhardt, had four wins in his '96 championship year, is out to better that total in '97.

NASCAR Craftsman Truck Race 3
Florida Dodge Dealers 400K
Homestead Motorsports Complex
Homestead, FL
March 16, 1997
167 Laps, 253.37 Miles

ROOKIE KENNY IRWIN RACES TO VICTORY CIRCLE AT HOMESTEAD

In only his third 1997 start, rookie Kenny Irwin, in the Raybestos Ford, displayed the speed and composure of a veteran to notch his first series victory. He took the lead from Jack Sprague with two laps to go and withstood intense pressure from runner-up Mike Bliss in the ASE Ford. The winning margin was a slim .289 of a second. Chuck Bown, in the Exide Ford, started third, finished the same way. 1997 inaugural race winner and today's polesitter, Joe Ruttman, led the first 38 laps, became a cropper for a lowly 26th place finish. Irwin, like 1995 Winston Cup champion Jeff Gordon, won titles in USAC's short track single seater series, is touted as a potential NASCAR star.

NASCAR Craftsman Truck Race 4
Chevy Trucks Desert Star Classic
Phoenix International Raceway
Phoenix, AZ
April 20, 1997
150 Laps, 150 Miles

JACK SPRAGUE SHINES AT PHOENIX

Once again Jack Sprague was on the pole and leading on the last lap with arch rival Joe Ruttman behind him. This time Ruttman couldn't get close enough to employ the bumping tactics that earned him victory at Disney World. Sprague's margin of victory was a huge 13.186 seconds. Third place Mike Bliss was the only other driver to get into the lead (from lap 36 through 77). Sprague led at the start and for the final 72 laps, was essentially unchallenged. Ron Hornaday failed in his victory quest, but a solid fourth place ahead of Rich Bickle in fifth, piled up useful points toward a repeat title. Early season indications are that Sprague and Bickle will provide strong opposition.

NASCAR Craftsman Truck Race 5
Craftsman 200
Portland Speedway
Portland, OR
May 3, 1997
200 Laps, 200 Miles

RICH BICKLE BLAZES THE WAY IN PORTLAND'S CRAFTSMAN 200

This time it was Rich Bickle's turn to win from the pole. Ron Hornaday, the second fastest qualifier, outjumped Bickle at the start to lead the first 43 laps. Bickle wrested the lead from Hornaday for the next 121 tours, lost it back, then regained it for the final 15 laps. His margin of victory was .675 of a second. Butch Miller nailed down third place. Lady driver Tammy Jo Kirk qualified her Lovable Ford third fastest, finished a respectable 14th just ahead of star rookie Kenny Irwin. Jack Sprague's fourth place kept him very much in the title chase. Rookie Tony Raines' seventh place in the Pennzoil Dodge, was a hint of better results to come.

NASCAR Craftsman Truck Race 6
NAPACARD 200
Evergreen Speedway
Monroe, WA
May 10, 1997
203 Laps, 131.138 Miles

RICH BICKLE MAKES IT TWO IN A ROW AT MONROE

Not only did Rich Bickle win his second race in a row, he again accomplished the feat from the pole. Although passed by second fastest qualifier Rick Carelli, in the RE/MAX Chevrolet, on lap two, he quickly got back in front and produced the race's highest number of laps in the lead, including the last 35. Carelli faded to a lap down at the end. Runner-up Jack Sprague came on strong to lead for 23 laps before Bickle took over for his final tour in front. Bickle's edge over Sprague was .319 second at the checker. Michael Dokken, in the DANA Corporation Dodge, was a solid third. Dodge drivers keep moving up in the points, knocking on victory's door.

Nigel Kinrade

Phillip Salazar

NASCAR Craftsman Truck Race 7
Western Auto/Parts America 200
I-70 Speedway
Odessa, MO
May 24, 1997
200 Laps, 108.6 Miles

ROOKIE TONY RAINES RIDES DODGE INTO VICTORY CIRCLE AT I-70 SPEEDWAY

It was a first for both of them, rookie driver Tony Raines and his Pennzoil Dodge mount. While Dodges had been fast in qualifying, until Raines' win, no driver had previously succeeded in carrying their speed all the way to the win column in the series. Raines gave warning early on. He qualified second fastest, outjumped polesitter Rich Bickle at the start and led for the first 56 laps. While Kenny Irwin, Jimmy Hensley, and Rich Bickle had sessions up front in between, Raines topped the chart for the final 92 laps. Hensley was second, .584 of a second in arrears, and Chuck Bown displaced Bickle for third.

NASCAR Craftsman Truck Race 8
Pennzoil VIP Discount Center 200
New Hampshire Intl. Speedway
Loudon, NH
May 31, 1997
200 Laps, 211.6 Miles

JAY SAUTER SURGES TO NEW HAMPSHIRE WIN

Coming from a way back 26th place starting slot, Jay Sauter, in the GM Goodwrench Chevrolet, made his mark on the New Hampshire mile oval. In a gritty performance, he caught up with polesitter Jack Sprague with only three laps to go and edged him by .571 seconds at the end. Runner-up Sprague led the first 115 laps and 57 more before Sauter got by on lap 198. Rick Carelli started even further back than Sauter, but made steady progress for a third place finish. The next three places were filled by rookies, Boris Said, Kenny Irwin and Rick Crawford indicative of the level of driving talent being drawn into the series. Rookie Tammy Jo Kirk finished on the lead lap.

NASCAR Craftsman Truck Race 9
Pronto Auto Parts 400
Texas Motor Speedway
Fort Worth, TX
June 6, 1997
167 Laps, 400 Kilometers

KENNY IRWIN GETS SECOND WIN OF '97 AT TEXAS

Kenny Irwin picked a good venue for his second win of the year, earning $58,950 in the rich Pronto Auto Parts 400 at Texas Motor Speedway. Only two drivers led the race, polesitter Mike Bliss, in the ASE Ford, for 112 tours, and Irwin for the final 52. Bliss faded to fifth at the end, allowing Boris Said, in the Federated Auto Parts Ford, and Rick Crawford, in the Circle Bar Ford, into second and third places respectively. All three of the top finishers were rookies. A fourth place by Chuck Bown ensured that the top five finishers all drove Fords. Sixth place Bob Keselowski was the top Dodge driver, finishing just ahead of Chevrolet-mounted Dave Rezendes.

NASCAR Craftsman Truck Race 10
Loadhandler 200
Bristol Motor Speedway
Bristol, TN
June 21, 1997
200 Laps, 106.600 Miles

RON HORNADAY IN WIRE-TO-WIRE BRISTOL RUNAWAY

Ron Hornaday came back from a plague of early season misfortunes with a bang in Bristol's Loadhandler 200. He put his NAPA Chevrolet on the pole and was never headed. Runner-up Rich Bickle, in the Sears DieHard Chevrolet, was a sizeable 1.536 seconds behind at the end. Chevrolet drivers Jay Sauter and Rick Carelli took down the third and fourth spots. The 1996 champion turned in a virtuoso performance for the full 200 laps. Fouth place fell to Rick Carelli, the third fastest qualifier, while Boris Said, second fastest in qualifying, finished two laps down.

NASCAR Craftsman Truck Race 11
NAPA AutoCare 200
Nazareth Speedway
Nazareth, PA
June 29, 1997
200 Laps, 200 Miles

JACK SPRAGUE NOTCHES NAZARETH WIN

It took Jack Sprague only 15 laps to get in front from his third starting position in Nazareth's NAPA AutoCare 200, displacing polesitter and early leader Mike Skinner. More importantly, he was in front for the final 33. Ron Hornaday and Joe Ruttman also had tours on top of the field with Ruttman edging Mike Bliss for runner-up honors. Second fastest qualifier Rich Bickle earned the fourth finishing position but never posted a lead lap. Hornaday ended up two laps down. Sprague set a new race record average (92.308 mph) but qualifying honors remained with Jimmy Hensley at 128.027 mph.

NASCAR Craftsman Truck Race 12
DieHard 200
The Milwaukee Mile
West Allis, WI
July 5, 1997
200 Laps, 200 Miles

RON HORNADAY ON TOP IN HOTLY CONTESTED DIEHARD 200

Only three drivers managed to lead in the DieHard 200 on the Milwaukee Mile but between them they produced 10 lead changes and excitement to spare for the fans. In the lead change that counted, Ron Hornaday took over from Jack Sprague, the polesitter, with three laps to go. Jay Sauter and Rich Bickle got past Sprague, too, as he dropped to fourth place at the end. Bickle was the third driver to lead, having two tours in front. Hornaday set a new track record of 105.665 mph in the process of winning by 1.055 seconds.

Nigel Kinrade

Nigel Kinrade

NASCAR Craftsman Truck Race 13
Link-Belt Construction Equip. 225
Louisville Motor Speedway
Louisville, KY
July 12, 1997
225 Laps, 98.55 Miles

RON HORNADAY ON A RAMPAGE, LEADS EVERY LAP AT LOUISVILLE

Ron Hornaday wasn't on the pole but he nosed his NAPA Chevrolet in front on the first lap and kept it there for every one of the 224 remaining in Louisville's Link-Belt 225. It wasn't quite a runaway; he was only .192 of a second ahead of runner-up Joe Ruttman, in the LCI Ford, at the end. Jimmy Hensley put the Cummins Engine Dodge on the pole, claimed third place at the finish. Talented rookie Tony Raines qualified second fastest in the Pennzoil Dodge, making it an all Dodge front row. He performed well in the race itself, finishing fourth, and claiming "Rookie of the Race" honors.

NASCAR Craftsman Truck Race 14
Colorado 250 by Snap-On Tools
Colorado National Speedway
Erie, CO
July 19, 1997
250 Laps, 93.75 Miles

RON HORNADAY CLAIMS THREE IN A ROW AT COLORADO

Ron Hornaday nailed down the pole position in qualifying but was outsprinted at the start by second fastest qualifier Mike Wallace in the Purolator Chevrolet. Hornaday didn't get his first tour in the lead until lap 65, taking over from Mike Bliss who ended up in second place. However, it was Hornaday's last session in the lead on lap 213 that counted. He easily ran out the remaining 37 for a handsome winning margin of 2.295 seconds. Third place went to rookie Stacy Compton in the Valvoline Ford. Championship contender Jack Sprague had a difficult day at the office, qualifying 21st and finishing 16th.

NASCAR Craftsman Truck Race 15
Lund Look 275K
Heartland Park Topeka
Topeka, KS
July 27, 1997
81 Laps, 170.10 Miles

JOE RUTTMAN PREVAILS ON HEARTLAND'S ROAD COURSE

Joe Ruttman, in the LCI Ford, proved to be the class of the field in the Lund Look 275K on Heartland Park's 2.1 mile road course. The action was fast and furious, with no less than seven drivers getting into the lead at some point in the proceedings. Polesitter Ruttman led the first four and the all-important last lap. Misfortune struck Jay Sauter, the leader on the penultimate lap, who ran out of fuel with the checker in sight. Jack Sprague, the runner-up, and third place Ron Hornaday were other beneficiaries of Sauter's bad luck. Trans-Am regular Dorsey Schroeder made a rare appearance and finished a creditable fourth.

NASCAR Craftsman Truck Race 16
Cummins 200
Indianapolis Raceway Park
Indianapolis, IN
July 31, 1997
202 Laps, 138.572 Miles

RON HORNADAY CLAIMS THE CUMMINS 200 AT IRP

Jimmy Hensley, appropriately driving the Cummins Dodge, appeared to have the Cummins 200 wrapped up. He was on the pole and led for 200 laps at Indianapolis Raceway Park. Unfortunately, the race called for 202 laps, allowing Ron Hornaday and Jack Sprague to sweep past. Hornaday got the winner's nod by .947 of a second. Sprague earned runner-up honors. A frustrated Hensley had to settle for third place.

NASCAR Craftsman Truck Race 17
Stevens Beil/Genuine Car Parts 200
Flemington Speedway
Flemington, NJ
August 9, 1997
200 Laps, 125 Miles

RON HORNADAY FLASHES TO FLEMINGTON WIN

Ron Hornaday swapped the lead with Tony Raines twice in the early going, bested the rookie on lap 21 and was never headed on his way to the checker in the Stevens Beil 200 at Flemington. Raines ended up out of the top 10. Runner-up Joe Ruttman was close at the finish, .313 of a second in arrears, followed by Rich Bickle. Surprise polesitter Terry Cook, in the PBA Tour Chevrolet, never led a lap, ended up a lap down.

NASCAR Craftsman Truck Race 18
Federated Auto Parts 250
Nashville Speedway USA
Nashville, TN
August 16, 1997
256 Laps, 152.576 Miles

JACK SPRAGUE SURGES TO NASHVILLE VICTORY

An on form Jack Sprague ran off the last 56 laps of the Federated Auto Parts 250 at Nashville in the lead and without serious challenge, his campaign for the drivers' title seemingly on course. Ron Hornaday, the second fastest qualifier, was .417 of a second behind at the finish, followed by Butch Miller. Polesitter Mike Bliss led the first 10 laps, ended up one lap down. Rookie Stacy Compton, in the Valvoline Ford, was a solid fifth, just behind Dave Rezendes in the Ortho Chevrolet.

Nigel Kinrade

Nigel Kinrade

NASCAR Craftsman Truck Race 19
Parts America 150
Watkins Glen International
Watkins Glen, NY
August 24, 1997
62 Laps, 151.9 Miles

ROAD RACER RON FELLOWS ON TOP AT WATKINS GLEN

Trans-Am standout Ron Fellows completed only 12 laps in the AER Chevrolet in his last truck outing at Heartland Park. This time he went all the way from the pole to the checker. Jack Sprague, in the Quaker State Chevrolet, was ahead for 39 laps in the middle but Fellows easily ran out the last four for a 1.401 second margin at the finish. Mike Bliss edged third place Sprague for the runner-up slot. Another Trans-Am regular, DorseySchroeder, the second fastest qualifier, lasted only 48 laps. Joe Ruttman, Ron Hornaday, and Jimmy Hensley followed the top three across the finish line.

NASCAR Craftsman Truck Race 20
Virginia Is For Lovers 200
Richmond International Raceway
Richmond, VA
September 4, 1997
200 Laps, 150 Miles

BOB KESELOWSKI AND DODGE THE VICTORS IN VIRGINIA

Bob Keselowski started back in the fifth row, but by mid-race he had forged his way up front and first took over the lead on lap 103 of the 200 scheduled. Jay Sauter, who eventually finished third, then intervened in the lead for 15 laps before Keselowski took over the top spot again on lap 173. His 3.056 second margin of victory was a clear indication of his superiority in the Mopar Dodge. Jack Sprague was the runner-up, while polesitter Ron Hornaday finished a lap down and out of the top 10. Rich Bickle garnered the fourth finishing slot with rookie Kenny Irwin finishing fifth.

NASCAR Craftsman Truck Race 21
Hanes 250
Martinsville Speedway
Martinsville, VA
September 27, 1997
256 Laps, 134.656 Miles

RICH BICKLE HUSTLES TO VICTORY IN THE HANES 250

Polesitter Rich Bickle, in the Sears DieHard Chevrolet, had a formidable foe alongside him in the front row in the Hanes 250 at Martinsville, none other than Winston Cup star Ernie Irvan, in the Federated Ford, who qualified second fastest. Irvan outjumped Bickle at the start, led for the first 52 laps. Bickle got by on lap 53 and Irvan's best efforts to dislodge him for the lead failed. The dueling pair, ended up the way they started with Bickle in front by .573 of a second. Mike Bliss, third on the starting grid, kept things tidy by finishing third. Winston Cup regular Bobby Hamilton took down fifth place behind Jimmy Hensley.

NASCAR Craftsman Truck Race 22
Kragen/Exide 151
Sears Point Raceway
Sonoma, CA
October 5, 1997
60 Laps, 151.20 Miles

JOE RUTTMAN ON TOP AT SEARS POINT

Joe Ruttman, in the LCI Ford, displayed his road racing talents to advantage on the tricky Sears Point circuit, winning by a comfortable 1.451 seconds over Tom Hubert in the DANA Dodge. Boris Said and polesitter Dave Rezendes swapped the early lead, but both ended up four laps off the pace. Jay Sauter ran a consistent race from his third fastest qualifying spot to finish third. Hubert was the surprise of the race, qualifying fourth, leading 13 laps in mid-race, and easily notching second place at the end. Jack Sprague qualified second fastest and finished in fifth place to gain some useful points.

NASCAR Craftsman Truck Race 23
Dodge California Truck Stop 300
Mesa Marin Raceway
Bakersfield, CA
October 12, 1997
300 Laps, 150 Miles

RANDY TOLSMA TAKES HIS FIRST WIN AT MESA MARIN

Starting position 13 was anything but bad luck for Randy Tolsma in the IWX/Dole Chevrolet. By mid-race he was up with the leaders, taking over the point from Ron Hornaday on lap 154. Hornaday and Tolsma then traded places - twice. Polesitter Mike Bliss and Mike Wallace had their turns on top but the last three laps were Tolsma's. Rookie Stacy Compton edged Bliss for the runner-up spot, with Jay Sauter close behind Bliss for fourth at the end. Tolsma's narrow margin of victory, .204 of a second, in no way detracted from his joy on winning for the first time in the series.

NASCAR Craftsman Truck Race 24
The No Fear Challenge
California Speedway
Fontana, CA
October 18, 1997
100 Laps, 200 Miles

MIKE BLISS BREEZES TO VICTORY IN RICH CALIFORNIA SPEEDWAY INAUGURAL

Mike Bliss earned a handsome $74,400 for his dominating win from the pole in California Speedway's No Fear Challenge. Jack Sprague outjumped Bliss on the first of 100 laps contested on the handsome two mile layout, and Ernie Irvan and Chuck Bown led for a handful of laps. However, by mid-race, Bliss was clearly in command, rolling off the final 54 laps for a comfortable 1.630 second margin over runner-up Mike Wallace at the end. Rookie Kenny Irwin placed third, ahead of fourth place finisher Irvan.

Nigel Kinrade

NASCAR Craftsman Truck Race 25
GM Goodwrench/Delco Battery 300
Phoenix International Raceway
Phoenix, Az
November 1, 1997
186 Laps, 186 Miles

JOE RUTTMAN GARNERS THE VICTORY AT PHOENIX

Rebounding Joe Ruttman came back from a disappointing performance at California to the winner's circle at Phoenix. Starting seventh, he moved up steadily, edged his LCI Ford in front on lap 131 of the 186 scheduled. Thereafter, he was not severely challenged, crossing the finish line with a .419 second margin. Jack Sprague, the strong man of the race's first two-thirds was beaten for runner-up honors by Chuck Bown. Rookie Kenny Irwin, a two-time winner in the series, had his best recent result, a strong fourth place.

Nigel Kinrade

NASCAR Craftsman Truck Race 26
CarQuest Auto Parts 420K
Las Vegas Motor Speedway
Las Vegas, NV
November 9, 1997
175 Laps, 262.5 Miles

JOE RUTTMAN ROLLS TO VICTORY CIRCLE IN LAS VEGAS' RICH FINALE

Las Vegas is all about money. So it was fitting that Joe Ruttman's purse for his win in the CarQuest 420K at Las Vegas Motor Speedway was a whopping $83,000, the largest offered in the series. He earned it, coming up from eighth place at the start and gaining the lead only three laps from the end. He was a full 1.512 seconds ahead of runner-up Quaker State Chevrolet driver Jack Sprague, the polesitter, and twice the race leader, at the finish. Sprague had ample consolation, he nailed down the Driver's Championship in the series and its near quarter million dollar bonus. Ron Hornaday notched third place.

Nigel Kinrade

DRIVERS

Alex Zanardi, Target/Ganassi's Comeback Kid

By David Phillips

It's not like Alex Zanardi didn't give the opposition a fighting chance. The preseason favorite to win the 1997 PPG Cup, Zanardi spotted Paul Tracy, Greg Moore, Michael Andretti, Gil de Ferran and Jimmy Vasser the first half of the season before getting his championship drive into high gear. Even then his largesse continued.

At Cleveland and Michigan, he advanced to the back of the field after running afoul of the rule book, yet won both races handily. Two more wins at Mid-Ohio and Road America sent Zanardi to Vancouver with a chance to clinch the title. Instead, he finished fourth after another comeback drive that left a string of bruised egos - and some fiberglass chips - in its wake. He wrapped up the title at Laguna Seca a week later. Good thing, as a pair of 230 mph practice crashes rendered him hors de combat for the season finale at California Speedway.

Along with Target/Ganassi Racing, Zanardi pulled into the Metro-Dade Homestead Motorsports Complex for the start of the season on a roll, with two wins and four poles from the final four races of 1996. He promptly re-established his credentials by taking his fifth straight pole and leading the early stages of the race before an assortment of problems, ranging from a handling imbalance to the loss of his rear mirrors, dropped him to seventh.

In Australia, Zanardi earned his sixth consecutive pole to establish a new CART record but tangled with Paul Tracy while disputing the lead and fell to 17th place. In a preview of things to come, Zanardi drove like a man possessed over the final 13 laps to climb back to fourth at the finish. When he scored his first victory of the season a week later in Long Beach, pressuring de Ferran, then taking the lead on the strength of superb pit work, it seemed the die was cast for 1997.

Zanardi struggled for the next two months, however, earning fourths at Rio and Gateway, two points at Nazareth and going pointless altogether at Milwaukee. After he was punted out at Detroit, then mistimed the critical switch to slick tires at rainy Portland, he fell all the way to sixth in the standings.

But Zanardi had the competition right where he wanted it. He took his third pole at Cleveland and led until a full course yellow. Zanardi failed to see the sign indicating the pit lane was closed and dove into the pits on lap 22, with a host of others following suit. For their indiscretions, Zanardi et al were given stop-and-go penalties, dropping them to the end of the lead lap. Not content with putting himself behind the eight ball, Zanardi incurred another penalty for improperly blending-in with the field upon his return to the track.

Unfazed, the plucky Italian scythed through the field like the proverbial hot knife through butter, setting consecutive fastest laps before outbraking de Ferran to regain the lead six laps from the finish.

After shadowing an on-form Mark Blundell home in Toronto, Zanardi used a variation on the Cleveland theme to return to victory lane in the U.S. 500 and assume the lead in the PPG Cup points race. This time, Zanardi was penalized for running over an air hose on pit lane. And while his comeback had the same result as his Cleveland recovery, this time Zanardi was aided by a slew of crashes and mechanical failures that eliminated other contenders. The result was the largest margin of victory of 1997 (31.7 seconds) over second place finisher Blundell.

The Italian went on to earn his second straight win at Mid-Ohio and then led Mauricio Gugelmin home in a rain-delayed Texaco 200 at Road America. When Zanardi beat Bobby Rahal for the pole at Vancouver, a notoriously difficult track on which to pass, it appeared the CART title was his for the taking.

But Zanardi never likes to make things easy. After leading the opening laps, fading brakes got the better of him and he sailed down the escape road in turn three. He immediately set about repeating his Cleveland and Michigan comebacks. He might have done it, but while running fourth on lap 83 he took another trip down the escape road. He returned to action again and, in the most controversial moment of the season, banged wheels passing race leader Bryan Herta. Herta wound up in the tire wall and Zanardi not only regained the lead lap but made up most of another lap on the leaders during the ensuing full course yellow. Thus he ultimately finished fourth, having made at least two dozen passes for position during the race.

CART officials, however, were unimpressed by his tactics, and subsequently fined him $25,000 and placed him on probation for the balance of the season.

A subdued but fiercely unrepentant Zanardi thus went to Laguna Seca knowing he needed only to finish ahead of de Ferran to clinch the PPG Cup. He did that easily, emerging unscathed from a few tense moments early in the race when he and Herta again tangled - albeit without recriminations - to come home third while de Ferran finished fifth.

Zanardi's was Target/Ganassi's second straight PPG Cup, coming hard on the heels of Jimmy Vasser's 1996 championship. The Californian endured an often frustrating title defense but

Steve Swope

finished the year impressively, with a win at Laguna Seca and seconds at Vancouver and California to vault to third in the standings after falling as far as seventh well into the season.

His resurgence apart, there were other bright spots to Vasser's season. He brought a less than perfect car home third at Homestead and was podium bound in Australia before Mauricio Gugelmin's uncharacteristic blunder knocked him out of contention. And he rebounded from an early puncture at Long Beach to come within a late full course yellow of victory.

Vasser also fared better on the short oval segment of the season than his teammate, but his string of 25 straight finishes came to a sad end at Portland when he was punted off the track in the closing laps. He subsequently struggled to find a good setup and often reverted to Zanardi's settings. Not until he and race engineer Julian Robertson reverted to their baseline settings from 1996 did Vasser mount his powerful stretch drive.

In contrast, Gil de Ferran began the season and his new association with Walker Racing in discouraging fashion, crashing no fewer than five cars in the first three weekends. At least he was running up front when he crashed though. After some soul searching in the wake of an unforced error at Long Beach, he developed into 1997's most consistent performer. Beginning with a fourth place at Nazareth, de Ferran finished in the points in 13 of the season's 14 final races, a DNF caused by a jammed throttle at Toronto, the only flaw on his record.

Unfortunately, he failed to score a victory, although he finished just .027 of a second behind Blundell in the rain and mist at Portland. De Ferran also had the legs on everyone but Zanardi at Cleveland and made a strong recovery drive of his own at Michigan to make the podium. That he did all this on Goodyear tires in a year in which Firestone drivers took eight of the top 10 spots in the points is all the more impressive and bodes well for 1998. Goodyear is unlikely to take these numbers lying down.

Few would argue that PacWest Racing has truly gotten its act together, as Mauricio Gugelmin and Mark Blundell placed fourth and sixth, respectively in the 1997 championship. Never once qualifying outside the top 10, Gugelmin was a factor in nearly every race. It wasn't until PacWest gambled by trying to run Detroit on one pit stop that he was in position to win, however. But along with Blundell, Gugelmin ran out of fuel while leading the final lap. A week later he dominated the wet stages of the Portland race only to slightly misjudge the timing of his change to slicks as Blundell stormed to the team's maiden win.

After leading three of the next five events, Gugelmin was finally rewarded with a powerful yet typically restrained win at Vancouver and went on to set a new closed course qualifying record with a 240.942 mph run to the pole at California Speedway.

The win at California, however, went to Blundell who emerged as a powerful force just when it appeared as though he might be left behind. After an alternately tough and promising rookie season, Blundell was eclipsed by Gugelmin in the early races before a shake up within PacWest's engineering group righted his season. His drive at Portland defined the word "racer" as he tigered through the field to catch - and pass - de Ferran at the flag. A month later, he beat Zanardi in a two car duel through the streets of Toronto and, when he outmaneuvered Vasser on the high banks of California Speedway it only served to confirm his status among CART's elite drivers.

Paul Tracy, of course, has long been a member of that select group and, when he led the PPG Cup standings from April through July, it looked as though he would join the even more august circle of CART champions. However, his season disintegrated amidst a long hot summer as the Penske PC26-Mercedes proved uncompetitive on the road and street circuits, and a series of first lap mishaps at Mid-Ohio, Road America and Vancouver put paid to his title hopes. After the season, Tracy was canned by Roger Penske in favor of Andre Ribeiro, adding a sour coda to a year that had begun with a promising second at Homestead and featured a hat trick of short oval wins at Nazareth, Rio and Gateway.

At that, Tracy had a better season than teammate Al Unser Jr. Robbed of a couple of victories in 1996, Unser rarely got within sight of victory lane in a 1997 season in which he was regularly outpaced by Tracy and felled by an uncharacteristic run of mechanical failures on those occasions when he was competitive. That he made the podium just once - with a third place at Nazareth - and was the only driver in the top 15 not to lead a lap says it all about Unser's 1997 season, not a typical one for the active driver with the second highest career victory total.

Greg Moore, Michael Andretti and Scott Pruett managed not only to lead, but led laps that counted. Moore scored a breakthrough win at Milwaukee under intense pressure from Andretti in the final laps. A week later the tables were turned as it was Moore who stalked the fuel conscious PacWest entries, winning when first Gugelmin then Blundell ran dry on the last lap. However, the Player's/Forsythe Reynard earned just one finish in the points in July, August and September.

Andretti peaked even earlier, scoring an historic win at Homestead in the Swift 007.i-Ford's debut, the first victory for an American built chassis since 1983. He followed that up with a third in Australia and a fighting second at Nazareth, but had an unproductive summer - one troubled by spotty reliability - and fell out of contention. At that, he had a better year than teammate Christian Fittipaldi who suffered a broken leg in a colossal accident in Australia, then returned in dynamic fashion with a fourth at Portland. But he couldn't buy a break and was destined to score just one more top five finish.

Scott Pruett started the season like a potential champion. He survived scoring gaffes at Homestead and Australia to finish fifth and first, respectively, and when he came home third at Long Beach it moved him into the PPG Cup points lead. But he dropped off the map at mid-season, crashing at Gateway and Michigan, and staggering home ninth in the points.

Pruett's swoon mirrored that of Patrick Racing teammate Raul Boesel who threatened to win a couple of races early in the year - leading at Long Beach, Nazareth and Gateway - but never quite got it all together after a fine third at Portland, just .055 of a second behind Blundell.

Team Rahal's season was a case of so near yet so far, as Bryan Herta won pole and led Alex Zanardi through the opening laps at Mid-Ohio before a tire disintegrated. He suffered more tire woes while leading from pole at Laguna Seca, leaving his third place finish at Cleveland as his seasonal high water mark. Equally frustrated was team leader Bobby Rahal who ran out of fuel a lap and a half from the finish at Rio while leading. Later he was on the pace in the U.S. 500 but found himself moved into the marbles in traffic and crashed. He finished third on the home ground at Mid-Ohio for his only podium finish.

Andre Ribeiro, Patrick Carpentier and Dario Franchitti were also more competitive than their respective finishes in the PPG Cup points would suggest. Ribeiro struggled with the Lola T97/00 before a mid-season switch to a Reynard revitalized his campaign. He finished a fine third at Toronto and dominated segments of the 500 mile races. A competitive, indeed potentially winning, driver on the ovals, Carpentier was off the pace elsewhere. But for a few gallons of fuel he'd have brought car owner Tony Bettenhausen his first victory at Gateway. He also led at Michigan only to fall out with transmission trouble. Still, he won the Rookie of the Year award thanks, in part, to the fact that Franchitti and Hogan Racing had an even worse finishing record. The ex-Mercedes touring car ace emerged as a front runner at Gateway and was usually to be found at the front of the field for the rest of the season, most notably in Toronto where he won the pole, only to get nudged off in a turn one fracas with Bobby Rahal.

Worse yet were the trials and tribulations of Adrian Fernandez, Richie Hearn and Parker Johnstone. Like Ribeiro, Fernandez was saddled with the Lola T97/00. Unlike his Tasman teammate, Fernandez was unable to marshall the finances to acquire a Reynard at mid-season. Thus, he plugged along in the Lola to little effect until a revised aerodynamic package transformed the car into a competitive proposition at California, the result being a fine third place. By then, Hearn and Della Penna Racing had already switched from their Lola to a Swift chassis, only to crash in practice. The former Toyota Atlantic champion thus had to look at ninth place at Gateway as his best finish of a difficult season.

Although Johnstone scored more consistently than Fernandez or Hearn, 1997 was nonetheless a major disappointment for the amiable Oregonian. Driving the favored Reynard-Honda-Firestone package for vaunted Team KOOL Green, Johnstone might have finished on the podium at Homestead but for confusion over CART's restart procedures. A fighting fifth at Long Beach served to confirm the potential, but instead only flattered to deceive. Johnstone fell off the pace as the season matured and a string of points paying finishes owed more to reliability than pace.

In contrast, while Michel Jourdain earned just one point for his efforts - a 12th at Portland - the young Mexican improved by leaps and bounds during the season to earn STP's Most Improved Driver award. Gualter Salles also showed signs of real promise in a rookie season with Gerald Davis' equally new outfit, and was rewarded with a seventh place run at Laguna Seca.

Slow progress by Toyota's engine program limited the efforts of Arciero-Wells drivers Max Papis and Hiro Matsushita, and their counterparts at All American Racers, Juan Fangio and P.J. Jones. Ironically, some of their best finishes came in long distance races at Michigan and California, with Papis leading Matsushita home in eighth in the U.S. 500 and Jones scoring his lone point of the year in the season finale.

Long gone from the scene at California Speedway when P.J. finished were Arnd Meier and Arie Luyendyk. The young German finished a difficult rookie season with the Project Indy team by collecting the two-time Indy 500 winner, who was driving in place of the injured Zanardi. Project Indy's best finish came at Michigan where Dennis Vitolo brought the team's Lola home in sixth; earlier in the season Project Indy co-owner Christian Danner had once again scored points at Detroit with a 12th place finish... driving for Payton-Coyne Racing.

Firehawk Racing Slick *Firehawk SS10 Street Tire*

Original Firehawk Indy Racing Rain Tire *Firehawk SZ50 Ultra-High Performance Tire*

Dan Bianchi

1 On Target... Alex Zanardi, taking aim at the PPG Cup drivers' championship, hit the bull's-eye with five wins, four Marlboro poles, claimed the title despite missing the last race. (195 PPG Cup points)

Steve Swope

2 Podium Perennial... Gil de Ferran notched no victories, but seven podium appearances and two Marlboro poles earned him the clear cut runner-up slot. (162 PPG Cup points)

Cheryl Day Anderson

3 '96 Champion... Jimmy Vasser was the hottest driver on the circuit late in the season, too late, however, to earn a second title. For his Target/Ganassi team it was a repeat of 1996, first and third in the points. (144 PPG Cup points)

Bob Steig

4 Fastest Lap Ever... Mauricio Gugelmin posted a closed course competition record of 240.942 mph to take the Marlboro pole at the new California Speedway. Two additional pole positions and a single victory propelled him into the year's top five. (132 PPG Cup points)

Dan Bianchi

5 Turbulent Season... Paul Tracy's three victories and two Marlboro poles were insufficient to gain him a contract renewal for 1998. His period of unemployment was short. (121 PPG Cup points)

Cheryll Day Anderson

6 Talent Rewarded... Mark Blundell shook off his rocky rookie season of ‘96 to score three victories, narrowly missing a fourth. (115 PPG Cup points)

7 Back-to-Back Winner... Greg Moore was in the thick of the title battle in the season's first half with consecutive wins and a pair of second places, lost momentum in the second half. (111 PPG Cup points)

Cheryl Day Anderson

8 Swift Start... **Michael Andretti**, the winningest active CART Indy car driver, made the new Ford-powered Swift chassis a winner the first time out, failed to crack victory lane again in '97. (108 PPG Cup points)

Dan Bianchi

9 On Top Down Under... **Scott Pruett** prevailed in Australia's Sunbelt IndyCarnival, notched two Marlboro poles to maintain his status as a front runner. (102 PPG Cup points)

Dan Bianchi

10 Upward Momentum... Raul Boesel notched the Marlboro pole at the new Gateway International Speedway, made a single podium appearance (at Portland) to secure membership in the elite top 10 club. (91 PPG Cup points)

Bob Steig

11 Fast, Not Fortunate... **Bryan Herta** once again demonstrated his speed with two Marlboro pole positions but his first win eluded him again. (72 PPG Cup points)

Steve Swope

12 Winding Down a Brilliant Career... Bobby Rahal, CART's only owner-driver and a three-time champion, missed the top 10 for the first time ever, announced his departure from the driver ranks at the end of the 1998 season. (70 PPG Cup points)

Dan Bianchi

13 Disappointing '97... Al Unser Jr., a two-time champion, failed to lead a single lap for the first year since his full time debut as an Indy car driver in 1983. Still considered the "ultimate" Indy car driver at 35, he's poised to take full advantage of an all new Penske chassis for '98. (67 PPG Cup points)

Dan Bianchi

14 Moving On in '98... Andre Ribeiro failed to match his two victory '96 performance but his 135 lead laps demonstrated continued talent. He was snapped up for '98 by blue chip Marlboro Team Penske. (45 PPG Cup points)

Steve Swope

15 Swift Recovery... Christian Fittipaldi had his potentially brilliant sophomore season interrupted by a serious crash, missed seven races, returned with speed and verve intact. (42 PPG Cup points)

Dan Bianchi

16 Opportunity Missed... Parker Johnstone, nominated for the top drawer Team KOOL Green ride in 1997, was unable to match the front running promise of his first two years on the circuit. (36 PPG Cup points)

17 Rookie of the Year... **Patrick Carpentier**, the 1996 Toyota Atlantic champion, easily made the transition to the PPG Cup series, came close to winning in his first year. (27 PPG Cup points)

Cheryl Day Anderson

Bob Steig

18 Lower Point Tally... **Adrian Fernandez** made his single podium appearance of '97 at California Speedway's season ending Marlboro 500 but lacked the sparkle of his '96 season, which included a win. (27 PPG Cup points)

Dan Bianchi

19 Talented Substitute... **Roberto Moreno** displayed a remarkable ability to hop into an unfamiliar car, qualify and perform creditably in the race. He subbed for injured Christian Fittipaldi. (16 PPG Cup points)

20 Promising Rookie... **Gualter Salles** showed competitive flair and managed to lead a single lap in his PPG Cup debut. (10 PPG Cup points)

Cheryl Day Anderson

David Taylor/Allsport

Blond and bearded Paul Tracy goes over test results with Team KOOL Green engineer.

Jamie Squire/Allsport

Swift sophomore Dario Franchitti looks for his first PPG Cup victory in '98.

Expanded Outlook for Team KOOL Green

Team KOOL Green lifted its sights for '98, naming proven race winner Paul Tracy and pole-winning '97 rookie Dario Franchitti to drive in its expanded two car team. Tracy posted three victories in a row in 1997, the year's second highest total (as well as a pair of pole positions). He ranks eighth on the all-time CART winners' list, ahead of such luminaries as Tom Sneva, Bobby Unser and Johnny Rutherford. Franchitti, a British Formula 3 champion under the tutelage of former World Champion and fellow Scotsman Jackie Stewart, came to Indy car racing highly recommended by Mercedes-Benz for whom he drove in various Touring Car series. In his rookie year on the PPG Cup circuit, he led four times for a total of 47 lead laps, justifying Mercedes' confidence. Team owner Barry Green hopes his new lineup has just the right blend of speed, experience and enthusiasm.

David Taylor/Allsport

Toyota Trio

All three Toyota-powered drivers, Dan Gurney's Juan Fangio II and P.J. Jones plus Arciero-Wells' Max Papis scored top 10 finishes in '97, but victory would have to wait til '98.

Dan Bianchi

Juan Fangio II

Dan Bianchi

Max Papis

Dan Bianchi

P. J. Jones

Steve Swope

PPG CART World Series Race 1
Marlboro Grand Prix of Miami
Presented by Toyota
Metro-Dade Homestead
Motorsports Complex
Homestead, FL
March 2, 1997
147 Laps, 1.517 Mile Oval

SWIFT '97 START FOR ANDRETTI IN THE MARLBORO GRAND PRIX OF MIAMI

Michael Andretti added to his stature as CART's winningest active driver by putting the new Ford-powered Swift chassis into the winner's circle the first time out. The Kmart/Texaco-Havoline standard bearer started in midpack, leaving polesitter Alex Zanardi and Gil de Ferran to battle for the lead. Andretti, moving up smoothly, garnered the lead at midpoint, when de Ferran tagged the wall. He relinquished it only for a few laps on a pit stop sequence. Outmatched in pure speed by Andretti, Zanardi suffered an additional misfortune, a jammed wheel nut resulting in an overly long pit stop which took him out of podium territory. He was left in the unhappy position of seventh at the end. Paul Tracy started third, finished second. He never posed a threat to Andretti's coming out party. Jimmy Vasser couldn't match his winning 1996 Homestead run, but posted a workmanlike third place in launching his bid for a second title in a row. Greg Moore, in Player's Indeck colors, served notice of winning potential by qualifying fourth fastest and finishing in the same slot. Two-time champions Bobby Rahal (down four laps at the end) and Al Unser Jr. (out with electrical bothers) were well off the pace. After the fall of the checkered flag the major question in the paddock was, "If Andretti and Swift can dance through the opposition on their first date, what happens when they really get to know each other?"

Steve Swope

PPG CART World Series Race 2
Sunbelt IndyCarnival Australia
Surfers Paradise, Australia
April 6, 1997
57 Laps, 2.794 Mile Street Course

THE SUN SHINES ON SCOTT PRUETT AT SURFERS PARADISE

Alex Zanardi got the lion's share of pre-race attention by snaring his sixth consecutive Marlboro pole, by an eyelash from Paul Tracy. This set a new CART record, and the stage for an exciting first half duel, beloved by the fans, but benefiting neither driver. When this pair tangled, as it seemed inevitable that they would they did a big, if unwitting favor for ultimate winner Scott Pruett. Pruett, moving up smoothly from his seventh starting position, was waiting in the wings to take the lead for the final 16 laps. A downcast Zanardi was ready to bail out of his crash stranded car when course workers got him started. Luckily he didn't even lose a lap and was scored in fourth place at the end. The other half of the confrontation, Tracy, was less fortunate. He lasted only two laps after the incident. Rookie Arnd Meier, a part-timer on the circuit, will go down in the CART record books as a lap leader, for the two circuits following the Zanardi/Tracy tangle. Least fortunate of all the day's competitors was sophomore driver Christian Fittipaldi. He was struck from behind shortly after the fall of the green flag, hit the wall almost head on. Andretti's Newman/Haas teammate was lucky to incur only a broken leg, but would be out of action for more than half the season. The incident brought out the red flag and necessitated a restart. Player's/Forsythe's Greg Moore nailed down a close second place, while Michael Andretti's move from 11th place at the start to third at the finish, consolidated his lead in the PPG Cup points race over Pruett and Moore. 1996 Champion Jimmy Vasser, the third fastest qualifier, barely made the points paying list with a 12th place finish. Pruett's Ford-powered victory again demonstrated the desireability of staying out of trouble and being poised to take the measure of those who don't.

Cheryl Day Anderson

Cheryl Day Anderson

PPG CART World Series Race 3
Toyota Grand Prix of Long Beach
Long Beach, CA
April 13, 1997
105 Laps, 1.586 Mile Street Course

ALEX ZANARDI ZIPS TO HIS FIRST '97 VICTORY AT LONG BEACH

There would be no seventh Marlboro pole in a row for Alex Zanardi at the Toyota Grand Prix of Long Beach. Gil de Ferran, in the Valvoline Reynard Honda, nipped him for that distinction. More satisfying for the spirited Italian, however, there *was* his first appearance of the new year in victory circle. This time Zanardi tempered his speed with good judgement and didn't even have to pass anybody to nail down the lead. His Target-Ganassi crew handed it to him on lap 40 with a slick pit stop on his Reynard Honda. A model of consistency in '97, Scott Pruett brought the Brahma Reynard Ford home third, placing him on the podium for all three of the year's events to date, and escalating him into the PPG Cup lead with 44 points, over today's winner Zanardi (41) and Michael Andretti (35) who suffered handling problems and lasted only 70 laps. Al Unser Jr., a midfield starter, posted his best result of the new season with a fourth place finish. Long Beach ranks as one of his favorite courses, understandably since he has scored six victories there. Behind Unser, in fifth place, a high for the season, was Team KOOL Green's Parker Johnstone. After leading twice for a total of 26 laps, polesitter de Ferran gave in to handling problems after 93 laps. Jimmy Vasser led for 11 laps but faded to a finishing spot just inside the top 10; the day clearly belonged to teammate Zanardi.

Cheryl Day Anderson

PPG CART World Series Race 4
Bosch Spark Plug Grand Prix
Presented by Toyota
Nazareth Speedway
Nazareth, PA
April 27, 1997
225 Laps, 1 Mile Oval

PAUL TRACY TOPS THE FIELD AT NAZARETH FIRST '97 WIN FOR MARLBORO TEAM PENSKE

Paul Tracy is too quick to be kept out of victory circle forever and his '97 debut on top of the charts was an auspicious one, at team owner Roger Penske's Nazareth Speedway. Tracy's win was executed in convincing style. He took the Marlboro pole over Nazareth resident Michael Andretti, led 186 laps of the 225, contested including the final 141. Staying in front this consistently is no mean feat at Nazareth's swift one mile oval where the leaders go past the stands with neck-snapping swiftness. First row qualifier Andretti led 18 laps, finished as he started, in second place. To the delight of his legion of fans, the podium was rounded out by Marlboro Team Penske's Al Unser Jr., for a lineup of North American veterans, somewhat of a rarity in this era, when a majority of CART drivers are European or Latin American nationals. Rookie Patrick Carpentier qualified third fastest, indicating a smooth transition to ovals, and brought his Alumax Reynard Mercedes home within the points paying window. Andretti's runner-up slot gained him the top peg on the PPG Cup leader board with 51, followed by Pruett (47) and today's winner, Tracy (45). Alex Zanardi had his poorest outing of the new year, qualifying well down in 21st place and moving up to 11th at the end. Teammate Jimmy Vasser did better, making the day's top five behind Gil de Ferran. De Ferran was fourth at the start, fourth at the finish, never a factor for victory. Raul Boesel kept the nose of his Reynard Ford Cosworth out in front of the pack for 21 laps in the early stages, faded to eighth at the end. Tracy was clearly the day's best and made no mistakes on a track where the close conditions generated 10 caution flags.

PPG CART World Series Race 5
Hollywood Rio 400
Emerson Fittipaldi Speedway
Rio de Janeiro, Brazil
May 11, 1997
133 Laps, 1.864 Mile Oval

PAUL TRACY ROLLS AT RIO FOR TWO IN A ROW

Paul Tracy survived an early tangle with Roberto Moreno, the surprise second fastest qualifier, and a spin of his own on the restart, to catch a flying but fuel-starved Bobby Rahal two laps from the end. To call Tracy lucky and Rahal unlucky would be an understatement. Rahal was the Rahal of old, qualifying third fastest, taking the lead on the second lap, and posting no less than 102 laps in the lead until he ran out of fuel while clearly in command. Tracy must be commended for his strict application to a fast but frugal game plan that called for only two pit stops. Also economy-minded, Greg Moore, the only other driver to make do with two stops, landed in second place when Rahal ran out of methanol. Filling in handsomely for the injured Christian Fittipaldi in the Kmart Budweiser Swift Ford, Moreno was the talk of qualifying, but never recovered from his shunt, finishing out of the points. Scott Pruett nabbed third place, felt he could have done better. He blamed a faulty fuel strategy calling for four stops that often left him in the hurly burly of midpack. Mauricio Gugelmin put his Hollywood PacWest Reynard Mercedes on the pole before a sell-out "hometown" crowd, later put it into the fence on lap 57. Electrical problems in qualifying, which left him 26th on the starting grid, delayed but failed to stop hard charging Alex Zanardi. He was up to fourth at the finish. Paul Tracy's second win in a row put him atop the PPG Cup points lead with 65, ahead of Scott Pruett (61) and Zanardi (55).

Steve Swope

Cheryl Day Anderson

PPG CART World Series Race 6
Motorola 300
Gateway International Raceway
Madison, IL
May 24, 1997
236 Laps, 1.270 Mile Oval

PAUL TRACY TAMES GATEWAY FOR THREE IN A ROW

In a near repeat of his Rio victory, Paul Tracy slipped past a fuel-starved race leader with two laps to go to claim the checkered flag at the newly completed Gateway International Raceway. This time his victim was rookie sensation Patrick Carpentier, the Alumax standard bearer, who was forced to back off on the throttle in the closing count-down in order to make it to the finish. Even then, he barely did. Carpentier inherited the lead from another rapid rookie, Dario Franchitti, stopped by a failing gearbox. Raul Boesel, the Marlboro pole winner, lasted only a single lap in the lead, finished 14th. Perennial podium occupant Gil de Ferran motored all the way up to third from his midpack starting position. Michael Andretti, running in the lead after the halfway point that determines an official race, made a bet the sprinkles, then prevailing, would turn to rain and the race would be called with him the winner. He lost when the weather cleared. All the other leaders had pitted on yellow and he was forced to make a green flag stop. Andretti ended up outside the top 10. Target-Ganassi teammates Alex Zanardi and '96 Champion Jimmy Vasser finished in tandem, fourth and fifth respectively. Tracy overcame a lap in arrears, attributable to an early pit stop on green, when the other leaders had stopped earlier on yellow.

Once again, pit stop strategy played a major role in the outcome, with Tracy strong enough to overcome an early miscue. His 85 PPG Cup points put him solidly in the lead over Zanardi (67) and Pruett (61). Accident victim Pruett earned no points today.

Dan Bianchi

PPG CART World Series Race 7
Miller 200
The Milwaukee Mile
West Allis, WI
June 1, 1997
200 Laps, 1.032 Mile Oval

GREG MOORE WINS IN WISCONSIN, HIS FIRST FOR PLAYER'S/FORSYTHE

Only two drivers were able to lead the pack in the Miller 200, the long standing PPG CART event on the Milwaukee Mile. Marlboro pole-sitter Paul Tracy was going for his fourth consecutive victory, which would have tied Al Unser Jr.'s record. Greg Moore was going for his first win ever. Moore got the nod on the basis of a perfectly executed two stop fuel strategy that left his Mercedes engine sputtering on the victory lap after his hard fought win. Tracy's third pit stop dropped him to sixth at the end. Michael Andretti, on a good run up to second place, probed Moore for any weakness in the closing laps, found none, settled for the runner-up slot. Bobby Rahal, who nearly tangled with Moore on their second pit stops, once again ran out of fuel just short of the finish. Jimmy Vasser posted a third place to keep his hopes of a repeat PPG Cup alive. Although Alex Zanardi was running well at the end, posting the race's fastest lap on lap 198, he didn't qualify well and finished down in 13th place, out of the points for the first time in '97. Tracy left the fray with the PPG Cup lead at 94 points, followed by Andretti (70) and Zanardi (67). Winner Moore was a close fourth at 65.

PPG CART World Series Race 8
ITT Automotive Detroit Grand Prix
Belle Isle Park
Detroit, MI
June 8, 1997
77 Laps, 2.1 Mile Street Course

DETROIT DRAMA STARS GREG MOORE IN LEADING ROLE PLAYER'S/FORSYTHE TEAM GETS TWO IN A ROW

Only one leading lap counts; the last one, which is exactly the strategy that Greg Moore's Player's/Forsythe team successfully deployed for the second race in a row. That strategy, and Moore's polished driving in the ITT Automotive Detroit Grand Prix, made him the youngest ever two-time winner in a single season in the history of CART. By taking a risky one-stop gamble on fuel, PacWest teammates Mauricio Gugelmin and Mark Blundell appeared to have the race won over Moore, trying hard in third place. Incredibly on the last lap, first leader Gugelmin, and then, on the last turn, second place teammate Mark Blundell coughed to a stop with empty tanks. In another masterful ride, this time from sixth place at the start, Michael Andretti again took down runner-up honors. His 86 PPG Cup points gained ground on idle leader Paul Tracy (94) who withdrew from the event with neck muscle spasms leading to mild vertigo. Double winner Moore moved into third place in the standings with 85 over today's fourth place finisher Jimmy Vasser (69). Detroit's Marlboro polesitter, Gil de Ferran, made the podium's third slot. In 1998, the CART contingent will drive on a longer, wider, faster Belle Isle circuit, the product of a substantial investment by organizer IMG.

Cheryl Day Anderson

Cheryl Day Anderson

PPG CART World Series Race 9
Budweiser/G.I. Joe's 200
Presented by Texaco-Havoline
Portland, OR
June 22, 1997
78 Laps, 1.967 Mile Road Course

MARK BLUNDELL EDGES GIL DE FERRAN IN PORTLAND

In CART's closest ever finish, the winner's margin a mere .027 second, Mark Blundell recovered from disappointment in Detroit to triumph in Portland. The Britisher's first PPG Cup victory came at the expense of Gil de Ferran, whom he bested in a drag strip run out of the last turn on the last lap. So close was the finish that, had it gone a football field length further, third place Raul Boesel might have prevailed. Where fuel strategy played a dominant role in the previous two events, tire strategy was the key to today's outing. A light rain prevailed all morning, and at the start, leading to puddles all around the circuit. The puddles were hazardous enough to justify a full course yellow from lap 18 until lap 24. On the next lap, the rain stopped and the guessing game as to if and when to go to slicks instead of the grooved rain tires on every car at the start began. Blundell's PacWest crew switched to Firestone slicks on lap 69 and seemed to have made just the right call as their driver outsprinted Goodyear rain tire equipped Gil de Ferran on the final straight. Paul Tracy came in for Goodyear slicks on lap 63 as did Gugelmin for Firestone slicks on lap 66. Their timing appeared premature since both spun off, but were able to continue. Marlboro polesitter Scott Pruett was unable to maintain his pace in the race, finished out of the points paying window.

Tracy's seventh place today was good for six PPG Cup points and a total of 100, tops for the season to date. Greg Moore's fifth place finish gave him a runner-up total of 95, ahead of Andretti with 91. The PacWest team was understandably jubilant at Blundell's win. The likeable ex-Formula One driver had suffered a harsh introduction to CART racing in his rookie '96 year and the frustration of his oh so near miss in Detroit last time out.

Motorsports Marketing at a Championship Level
ITT Automotive Detroit Grand Prix
June 5 - 7, 1998
Medic Drug Grand Prix of Cleveland
July 10 - 12, 1998
IndyCarnival, Australia
October 15 - 18, 1998
IMG
IMG
IMG
ITT AUTOMOTIVE
TARGET
HOGAN
IMG Motorsports
IMG Center, Suite 100, 1360 East 9th Street, Cleveland, Ohio, 44114-1782 • (216) 522-1200

PPG CART World Series Race 10
Medic Drug Grand Prix of Cleveland
Burke Lakefront Airport
Cleveland, OH
July 13, 1997
90 Laps. 2.106 Mile Road Course

ALEX ZANARDI CONQUERS CLEVELAND, DESPITE DUAL PENALTIES

It would have broken the heart and melted the resolve of most drivers - not Alex Zanardi. Having taken the Marlboro pole for Cleveland's Medic Drug Grand Prix he was cruising with a three second lead on lap 21, when an all course yellow came out to remove Richie Hearn's crashed Lola. Mistakenly believing the pits to be open (as did a half dozen other drivers), Zanardi darted into them for service. They weren't. Penalty; go to the back of the field. Darting out, Zanardi improperly blended into the field. Penalty; go through the pit lane under green. After this quick shift from first to 26th, most drivers would have been discouraged. With 59 laps to go he merely kept his right foot down and, without the benefit of any yellow flags, was up to second place behind Gil de Ferran, the second

Photos by Cheryl Day Anderson

fastest qualifier, with six laps remaining. He easily bested de Ferran, who edged him here in '96, for a clear cut 1.281 second margin of victory. De Ferran, conserving fuel, was not permitted the luxury of an all out defense of his lead, but it probably would have made little difference. Bryan Herta, who always runs well at Cleveland, earned the third podium position. Paul Tracy's seventh place today helped retain his perch atop the PPG Cup standings with 106 points. Michael Andretti and Greg Moore both had mechanical problems but Moore retained second place in the points with 95 while Andrett, at 91, was bumped from third place by Gil de Ferran with 94 points. Zanardi's 21 point production in Cleveland moved him into serious contention for the PPG Cup with a total of 90 and seven races left on the schedule.

Winning Portrait...
Target/Ganassi's Chip Ganassi, Alex Zanardi, Target's Bob Ulrich, and team co-owner Joe Montana celebrate a come from behind victory in Cleveland (above).

Steve Swope

PPG CART World Series Race 11
Molson Indy
Toronto, Ontario, Canada
July 20, 1997
95 Laps, 1.721 Mile Street Course

MARK BLUNDELL BLAZES HIS WAY TO TORONTO VICTORY

Mark Blundell and his Motorola PacWest team proved that their Portland victory was no fluke by leading every lap but two, including the last 60 in Toronto's Molson Indy. Blundell got the lead in the first turn when Marlboro polesitter Dario Franchitti and third fastest qualifier Bobby Rahal tangled at the entrance. He allowed only single lap tours in front by Greg Moore and Raul Boesel the rest of the afternoon. Even hard charging Alex Zanardi never seriously threatened and had to settle for runner-up honors. Franchitti was in a hurry, making up for lost time, when he overdid it on lap 40 and tagged the wall. Rahal recovered from his Franchitti tangle for a ninth place finish. Andre Ribeiro, in his first outing in a '97 Reynard, showed the speed that made him a two-time winner in '96, garnered the third podium place. Paul Tracy's 10th place today left him with a slim lead over surging Zanardi, 109 to 106. Today's fourth place finisher, Michael Andretti, left the circuit with 103 points, good for third place. Greg Moore, trying hard, tagged the wall on lap 70. No points at Toronto put him in fourth place with 95. Blundell's only serious problem in Toronto appeared to be getting past drivers about to be lapped.

TEAMS
Target/Ganassi on Top with Two Straight Titles

By David Phillips

The 1997 PPG CART World Series witnessed a changing of the guard among CART's powerhouse teams past, present, and future. Established powers like Marlboro Team Penske, Newman-Haas Racing, Patrick Racing, and Team Rahal suffered disappointing seasons even as Target/Ganassi Racing confirmed its pre-eminent position in today's pecking order with its second straight PPG Cup. Meanwhile, other teams like the PacWest Racing Group, Walker and Player's/Forsythe Racing staked their claims as teams of the future.

In 1997, Target/Ganassi became the first team to win back-to-back PPG Cups since Truesports Racing's double with Bobby Rahal in 1986-87. In contrast to Truesports, Target-Ganassi won its titles with two different drivers; Jimmy Vasser dominating the opening half of last season to take the '96 championship and Alex Zanardi dominating the second half of 1997 to make it two in a row.

One key to the team's success has been its stable line up of key personnel, headed by managing director Tom Anderson and team manager Mike Hull. Starring in this talented assemblage are Zanardi's race engineer Morris Nunn and crew chief Rob Hill. Not only did they consistently provide Zanardi with a winning car, their cracker jack pit work at Long Beach and Road America put him in position to win races. The team's Reynard-Honda-Firestone package again proved effective.

While Vasser enjoyed similar continuity with race engineer Julian Robertson and crew chief Grant Weaver, there were a number of new faces on the remainder of his crew and it took time for the new assembly to jell. Too, Vasser and Robertson were not on the same wave length for much of the season, but they came together in time to clinch third in the PPG Cup standings. Two consecutive third places on top of the two titles add another feather to the Target/Ganassi cap.

PacWest Racing was second biggest of 1997's success stories, earning its first four victories in CART competition, the year's runner-up team total. After running up front but failing to win in the first third of the year, team owner Bruce McCaw, team manager John Anderson and crew chief Russ Cameron gambled on a one stop fuel strategy at Detroit. It put Mauricio Gugelmin and Mark Blundell in the lead in the closing laps. Though they both ran shy of fuel on the final lap, Blundell rebounded with a dramatic win at Portland, followed by wins at Toronto and California Speedway while Gugelmin scored a win of his own at Vancouver.

The key to Blundell's season was a change in race engineers at Gateway that saw Jim Hamilton shift over to the team's R&D programs, enabling Allen McDonald to take charge of the Reynard-Mercedes-Firestone set-up. Back for his third season with race engineer Andy Brown, Gugelmin was on the pace right from the start and was rewarded for his efforts with a win at Vancouver and his astonishing 240.942 mph pole at California Speedway, the fastest closed course lap in history.

Walker Racing experienced a timely revival, thanks to the arrival of Gil de Ferran, race engineer Bill Pappas, and Honda engines. The team also established close ties with Reynard and Goodyear, that were to prove fruitful over the course of the season. The top Goodyear runner, de Ferran showed remarkable consistency and was the series runner-up. Team manager Ron Meadows and chief mechanic Dan Miller took full advantage of the team's downsizing to a one car operation. They guided de Ferran to a nearly flawless reliability run, one blighted only by a series of shunts early in the year and one mechanical DNF.

Consistent though they may have been, the Walker team never managed to win a race - falling just .027 of second short at Portland. On the other hand, while Player's/Forsythe and Greg Moore scored breakthrough wins at Milwaukee and Detroit, putting them in the thick of the points battle, consistency deserted the Tony Brunetti-managed team in the second half of the season. Moore and long time race engineer Steve Challis performed admirably, especially in light of the team's switch from Lola to Reynard-Mercedes-Firestone line up just before the start of the season. After a strong spring, a variety of problems took them out of the championship chase in the second half.

Similarly, it was a case of feast or famine for Marlboro Team Penske in 1997. Under the direction of general manager Chuck Sprague, team manager Tom Wurtz, and chief mechanic Cliver Howell, Penske fielded two Goodyear shod PC26 Mercedes for Paul Tracy and Al Unser Jr. After an excellent spring in which Tracy, race engineer Ian Reed, and crew chief Jon Bouslog scored three wins, the team lost its way and never saw another podium finish. Unser, race engineer Grant Newbury, and crew chief Rick Rinaman suffered a singularly disappointing season, often uncompetitive and seemingly destined to suffer mechanical problems in those races where they were on the pace.

Newman/Haas and Michael Andretti got the 1997 season off to a cracking start, scoring a win at Homestead in the debut of the Swift 007.i-Ford and scoring gobs of points with podium finishes in the first half of the season. As the season progressed, Andretti and race engineer Peter Gibbons struggled at times to

(continued on page IC 42)

PPG CART World Series Race 12
U.S. 500 Presented by Toyota
Michigan Speedway
Brooklyn, MI
July 27, 1997
250 Laps, 2 Mile Oval

ZANARDI MASTERS MICHIGAN'S HIGH BANKS IN THE U.S. 500

"Sure he's great on the road circuits, but he'll never win a 500 mile race on a superspeedway, too impatient," that was the prevailing paddock line on Alex Zanardi. Zanardi proved the pundits wrong by outlasting and outdriving a strong field over 500 miles on Michigan Speedway's blisteringly fast banks in 95° heat and humidity to match. Zanardi qualified respectfully, but well in arrears of Marlboro polesitter Scott Pruett and his teammate, third fastest qualifier Raul Boesel, both in Ford-powered Reynards. Mauricio Gugelmin used Mercedes-Benz power to take the second front row starting position, and the lead for 34 of the first 35 tours. In turn, Andre Ribeiro, Scott Pruett and Michael Andretti took over the lead. Pruett remained in the thick of the lead pack until hitting the wall on lap 175. Zanardi did a near repeat of his

Cleveland pit miscue on his first stop, running over teammate Jimmy Vasser's air hose and incurring, as a penalty, an extra green flag tour through the pit lane. It could have cost him the race, but it didn't. He assumed the lead on lap 119 of the 250 scheduled, the first of his three tours in front, which included the last 31 laps. His lead lap total of 114 was a measure of his dominance of the event.

Mark Blundell moved up steadily from his 11th starting position to finish second, without ever leading a lap. Dario Franchitti, Bobby Rahal and Patrick Carpentier all enjoyed stints in front with little to show for it at day's end; no points for the trio. Interestingly, Toyota-powered Max Papis and Juan Fangio II both produced points paying finishes.

In the end, it was clearly Alex Zanardi, by a handsome 31.737 second margin over Blundell, followed by Gil de Ferran. Zanardi assumed the PPG Cup points lead with 127, de Ferran (108) followed in third. Paul Tracy, A game fourth place finisher today, was demoted to second at 121. With four of the remaining five events on his favorite road circuits Zanardi would seem to have momentum on his side.

Steve Swope

come to grips with the new chassis, while the Tim Bumps-led crew suffered several DNFs associated with teething problems associated with an all new car.

Christian Fittipaldi missed much of the season after his crash at Surfers Paradise, opening the door for Roberto Moreno to join race engineer Brian Lisles and the John Simmonds-led crew for a half dozen races which produced a best finish of fifth at Detroit.

Team KOOL Green manager Kyle Moyer and chief mechanic Tony Cotman along with race engineers Tony Cicale and John Dick produced enviable reliability with the Reynard Honda package, but the combination of disappointing speed and a series of shunts left them out of contention for the title. Driver Parker Johnstone left at season end.

Team Rahal also suffered through a frustrating season, with both Bryan Herta and Bobby Rahal coming agonizingly close to victory on several occasions. The organization's personnel line up remained static, with Tim Cindric and Scott Roembke returning as team manager and general manager, respectively. However, the team again made a major change in the chassis-engine-tire package in the off-season - switching from Mercedes to Ford power. It took Bobby Rahal, Bryan Herta, and race engineers Tim Reiter and Ray Leto a few weekends to get up to speed, but Rahal came within a few gallons of methanol of victory at Rio and, later, Herta led impressively at Mid-Ohio and Laguna Seca.

Patrick Racing got off to a great start in 1997 in its new guise as the Brahma Sports Team, switching from Lola to Reynard chassis after the former's T97/00 proved inconsistent in pre-season testing. Under the veteran leadership of general manager Jim McGee, team manager Steve Newey, and crew chief Tony Van Dongen, the team never missed a beat in the first race of the campaign. Working again with race engineer Tom German and chief mechanic Don Lambert, Scott Pruett brought the team a win at Surfers Paradise and two more podium finishes early in the season. Meanwhile, new addition Raul Boesel teamed with race engineer John Ward and chief mechanic Don Sales to lead at Long Beach, Nazareth, and Gateway. However, victory again eluded the Brazilian and the team's Reynard-Fords rarely figured in the latter half of the year.

In contrast to Player's/Forsythe and Patrick, several other teams stuck with the Lola chassis through much of the season - to their regret. The "Slow-la" crippled Tasman Motorsports' efforts to capitalize on a 1996 season in which drivers Andre Ribeiro and Adrian Fernandez combined for three victories. Under the direction of owner Steve Horne and team manager Jeff Eischen the team struggled heroically with their Lola-Hondas before a mid-season switch to Reynard chassis revitalized Ribeiro's campaign. Working again with race engineer Don Halliday and chief mechanic Steve Ragan, Ribeiro earned a third place at Toronto and led at Michigan and California. Fernandez, alas, was stuck with the Lola and it wasn't until a revised aerodynamic pakcage arrived at California that he, race engineer Diane Holl, and chief mechanic Andy Jones reaped the rewards for a difficult season with a third place.

Payton Coyne Racing also made the switch to Reynards at mid-season, proving a springboard for Michel Jourdain Jr. to post a number of impressive performances, much to the delight of Dale Coyne, Walter Payton, and team manager Bernie Myers. Like Fernandez and Tasman, however, the Della Penna and Project Indy teams were stuck with the Lola and the results showed. In their first full CART campaign, John Della Penna and his crew, led by chief mechanic Phil Howard and race engineer David Cripps, were limited to a pair of ninth place finishes. Team owner Andreas Leberle, team manager Brian Nott, race engineer Keith Leighton and the Project Indy team struggled with their Lola, but they achieved a points paying reward, a 12th place finish at the U.S. 500.

On a brighter note, Team Alumax Bettenhausen enjoyed a number of good weekends with an all new line up featuring chief engineer and managing director Tom Brown who joined team manager Joe Ward and chief mechanic Paul Hartman for 1997. Rookie driver Patrick Carpentier came close to a couple of wins, most notably at Gateway. Despite being curiously off the pace on the road circuits, for a Toyota Atlantic graduate, he managed to capture CART's Rookie of the Year honors.

Carpentier's main competition for rookie honors came from Scotsman Dario Franchitti, a late addition to the series in Carl Hogan's Reynard Mercedes. Hogan had parted company with Roger Penske after a season together in 1996 and formed his own team featuring team manager Peter Scott and engineer Alan Langridge along with several members of the former Brix-Comptech team including general manager Doug Peterson and crew chief Shad Huntley. Franchitti set a blistering pace at times, but a series of driver and crew miscues repeatedly cost them good finishes.

Dan Gurney's All American Racers and Arciero/Wells Racing were once again limited by the pace of Toyota's development. By the end of the season they were showing signs of improved reliability and gains in speed sufficient to put some points on the board. AAR's dynamic driving duo of Juan Manuel Fangio II and P.J. Jones at least had the known quantity of Reynard chassis this year, having struggled with the Eagle MK V in 1996. Team manager Gary Donahoe and chief mechanic Gary Martin oversaw preparation of the twin Castrol sponsored entries while Matt Cranor headed up a technical group featuring race engineers Bernie Marcus and Gerald Tyler.

At Arciero/Wells, general manager Mark Johnson and team manager Richard Buck worked with veteran engineer Gordon Coppuck and versatile Ed Nathman on the technical side, while Bharat Naran and Brad Filbey oversaw mechanical preparation of the cars of Max Papis and Hiro Matsushita, respectively. Papis earned points at Detroit and California and also headed Matsushita home to an eighth-ninth showing in the U.S. 500, the team's best outing of the season.

Cheryl Day Anderson

PPG CART World Series Race 13
Miller 200
Mid-Ohio Sports Car Course
Lexington, OH
August 10, 1997
83 Laps, 2.25 Mile Road Course

ALEX ZANARDI MAKES IT TWO IN A ROW AT MID-OHIO

Alex Zanardi had a clear and trouble free run to his second consecutive victory on the rolling hillsides of Mid-Ohio. He didn't even have to pass Marlboro polesitter Bryan Herta, who led the first 18 laps handily until derailed by a deflating soft compound left rear tire. Herta teammate Bobby Rahal, taking a more conservative tack, elected to go with hard compound tires and was rewarded with a third place at the finish. On the first lap, Michael Andretti was tagged from behind. The shunt quickly involved Paul Tracy and Parker Johnstone. Tracy suffered the most damage and was out for the day. Andretti and Johnstone managed to produce points paying finishes. Third fastest qualifier Greg Moore patiently stalked leader Zanardi without ever being poised to pass. He accepted the runner-up position with a sigh of relief from the bad luck of his three previous out-of-the-points finishes. Zanardi's smooth run to the checker and 56 laps led netted him 21 PPG Cup points for a total of 148, well ahead of luckless Paul Tracy in second place with 121. Gil de Ferran's sixth place gave him a total of 116, ahead of Moore, now fourth in the standings with 111.

PPG CART World Series Race 14
Texaco-Havoline 200
Elkhart Lake, WI
August 17, 1997
50 Laps, 4.048 Mile Road Course

ALEX ZANARDI RACES TO THIRD VICTORY IN A ROW AT ROAD AMERICA

Rain looked like it might stop the Texaco-Havoline 200 at Road America. The puddles were so omnipresent and threatening that the start was delayed more than two hours. Once underway, nothing could stop Alex Zanardi, enroute to his third victory in a row, not even a pair of off course excursions. He wasn't alone in going off the pavement. In the middle of turn one Gualter Salles spun. Paul Tracy, behind him, unavoidably tagged Salles' spinning car. Luckless Tracy slithered into the tire wall and gently rolled over. "First time I've ever been on my head in my entire career," was Tracy's downcast observation of his second crash in two races, neither of which were of his making. The early lead alternated between teammates Mauricio Gugelmin, the Marlboro polesitter, and Mark Blundell, the second fastest qualifier. Then, Bryan Herta managed four laps in front before giving way to Blundell. Zanardi was a close second, with Gugelmin following. Blundell's lead was lost in the pits when the Ganassi team elected not to change tires, a move which allowed their driver to beat Blundell back on to the circuit. Once in front, Zanardi first widened his lead then saw it almost vanish when he went off into the grass a second time. Just as things were getting frantic up front, Blundell's gallant bid evaporated in low oil pressure and a small fire that left him off course and down three laps at the end. Gugelmin, now second, could mount no threat to Zanardi, who won with 6.148 seconds in hand. Gil de Ferran once more mounted the podium in third place. At day's end Zanardi (168 points) had moved his margin over de Ferran (130) up to 38 points. Paul Tracy soldiered along in the third spot with 121.

Cheryl Day Anderson

Cheryl Day Anderson

PPG CART World Series Race 15
Molson Indy Vancouver
Vancouver, British Columbia, Canada
August 31, 1997
100 Laps, 1.703 Mile Street Course

MAURICIO GUGELMIN WINS AT LAST, HIS LUCK TURNS AT MOLSON INDY VANCOUVER

Long delayed (it was his 67th PPG Cup start) and well earned (he had come agonizingly close before), Mauricio "Mo" Gugelmin finally scored his first victory in the series in the Molson Indy Vancouver. Gugelmin was ecstatic to lose the proverbial "40 pound monkey" off his back, and provide his fast rising PacWest team with its third victory of the year. Even so, he needed an assist from Marlboro pole winner and series points leader Alex Zanardi to turn the trick. Zanardi was comfortably in the lead until the first of two trips into the run-off area on lap 16, which allowed second fastest qualifier Bobby Rahal to take over. In typical comeback mode, Zanardi hustled up to fourth place from back in the pack before repeating his run-off escapade. By now, he was a full lap down. Undaunted, he charged back and, in an effort to unlap himself, knocked then leader Bryan Herta into the tire barrier. Herta, by now, could be forgiven for having nightmares involving Zanardi. After the race, CART gave the hard driving Zanardi something to think about, a $25,000 fine and a two race probation term. Earlier in the proceedings Zanardi's teammate Jimmy Vasser, the third fastest qualifier, had alternated in the lead with Bobby Rahal and Gugelmin. He settled for second place at the end, after Rahal's day ended with engine failure. Gugelmin's Brazilian countryman, Gil de Ferran, once again picked up third place. Despite his off course excursions and bumping incident, Zanardi somehow managed fourth place, good for a PPG Cup points total of 181 and an almost unassailable lead over second ranked Gil de Ferran at 144. Again unfortunate, Paul Tracy's second lap shunt with Raul Boesel left him without points for the day, mired in third place at 121 and out of the contest for the PPG Cup.

Cheryl Day Anderson

PPG CART World Series Race 16
Toyota Grand Prix of Monterey
Laguna Seca Raceway
Monterey, CA
September 7, 1997

IT'S TARGET/GANASSI DAY AT LAGUNA SECA AGAIN, VASSER WINS THE RACE, ZANARDI TAKES THE TITLE

Once again, Bryan Herta and arch rival Alex Zanardi were squared off in close quarters. Herta won the Marlboro pole with Zanardi alongside him in the other front row starting position. Once again, Zanardi prevailed, although he didn't win the race. In the first 21 laps, Zanardi made only one serious attempt to get by leader Herta, a failed one. On lap 22, he decided to "go for it," on the outside, got bumped into the dirt for his pains. Third place Scott Pruett was the beneficiary of this confrontation. He slipped by both for the lead. Jimmy Vasser got by Herta, who was struggling with worn soft compound tires, shortly thereafter. Pruett's lead lasted only four laps, at which point, Vasser beat him out of the pits. The next 58 laps, and victory, all belonged to Vasser. Pruett went out of contention on lap 80 after a tangle with Andre Ribeiro, who survived the incident to finish fourth. Through all this, fourth fastest qualifier Mark Blundell moved into a solid second place, which he retained to the end. He could make no legitimate move on leader Vasser, and third place Zanardi, with the title in hand was disinclined to make a move on him. Zanardi's post race total of 195 PPG Cup points gave him the title, irrespective of the final round results. Gil de Ferran's fifth place today made him a shoe in for the year's runner-up honors. If today's winner, Vasser, now at 128 points, can maintain his pace in the season ending Marlboro 500 at the California Speedway, he'll give Target/Ganassi a repeat of their 1996 results, first and third in the championship, with the two drivers' roles reversed. Target/Ganassi Racing already had one role reversal for the day. In '96, Zanardi won the race and third place for Jimmy Vasser gave him the PPG Cup. This remarkable record for the team flies in the face of series history which shows that winning a title is difficult enough, winning it twice in a row is a rarity.

Steve Swope

PPG CART World Series Race 17
Marlboro 500 Presented by Toyota
California Speedway
Fontana, CA
September 28, 1997
250 Laps, 2.029 Mile Oval

MARK BLUNDELL ON TOP IN THE MARLBORO 500, CART'S EXCITING 1997 FINALE AT CALIFORNIA SPEEDWAY

It was a wild weekend. The new PPG Cup Champion Alex Zanardi didn't even start the race. He tagged the wall twice in practice and had to sit it out with a mild concussion. His replacement, Arie Luyendyk, repeated the incident 39 laps into the race. Mauricio Gugelmin set a new world closed course record in qualifying for the Marlboro pole; 240.942 mph. A dozen other qualifiers recorded speeds over 235 mph. The big incident in the race was triggered when leader Greg Moore's engine blew in spectacular fashion on lap 240 of the 250 scheduled. Jimmy Vasser and Mark Blundell, following, slowed. Their first concern was their own safety, their next, the yellow flag anticipated. There was no yellow flag. Blundell and his crew took note of this condition earlier than did the Vasser camp. Blundell sailed by Vasser and that was the race.

As might be expected in a 500 mile race there was no scarcity of lap leaders. In addition to Moore, Gugelmin, Vasser, and Blundell, Richie Hearn, Michael Andretti, Andre Ribeiro, and Gil de Ferran all had tours in front. Ribeiro had the most laps in front, 114, and could have been a factor at the end had he not collided with the wall on lap 208. Adrian Fernandez was the surprise third finisher, while tire concerns cost Gugelmin his chance at victory, dropping him to fourth place at the end. Blundell's alertness, coupled with a fine drive, earned him the victory, his third of the season, capping an outstanding sophomore year.

TONY STEWART TAKES THE TITLE
Indy Racing League Makes Progress

Tony George's new Indy Racing League had a lot to digest in its first full year, new chassis, new normally aspirated engine formula, new drivers and teams, new oval tracks, even a new sanctioning body late in the season. There were a few hiccups, but the IRL did digest its new menu and came up with some colorful, competitve racing. So competitive that there were seven winners in the eight 1997 races. (The last two events of '96 run under the old formula counted for the championship in a transition year.)

One of the winners was Tony Stewart, generally conceded to be the most talented of the new IRL faces recruited from the ranks of short track drivers. He deservedly became the IRL's first full season champion. Stewart usually qualified well, taking half the eight 1997 poles contested, but couldn't manage a win until the year's fifth event, at Pike's Peak. He'd been close before, but had been frustrated by mechanical failure.

At that, his closest competitor in the points chase, Davey Hamilton, never finished higher than third but was more consistent than Stewart.

Onwer/driver Eddie Cheever, a CART and Formula One veteran, inherited a win at Disney World but lost a sure victory at New Hampshire when his gearbox failed three laps from the end, while owning a comfortable lead. He tied for third place in the points campaign with winless Marco Greco, the New Hampshire polesitter. Greco's best finish was fourth.

Fifth place Scott Goodyear missed the '96 events, and, more importantly, narrowly missed a victory in the Indianapolis 500 for the second time in his career. This time, an officiating gaffe may have cost him the lucrative win.

Veteran Arie Luyendyk won two of 1997's eight races, including the big one at Indianapolis for the second time. This was the high point of a season which ended in sixth place in the points chase. A scoring miscue that failed to credit him with two laps led to his invasion of the Texas winner's circle, occupied by USAC's announced winner, Billy Boat, and his car owner AJ Foyt. It also led to Foyt's punching of Luyendyk. The incident failed to add lustre to the new league and its USAC sanctioning body.

Roberto Guerrero, who was handicapped by his team's choice of Nissan power at the start of the season, still managed to take down seventh place in the points.

Buddy Lazier, the courageous 1996 Indianapolis 500 winner, had to settle for fourth in the 1997 500. He did claim the victory at Charlotte in IRL's invasion of NASCAR territory. His season total was good enough for eighth at year end.

Eliseo Salazar was the year's comeback star. He broke his back in a pre-season testing accident, and missed two races. He courageously came back, regained form, and won the year end Las Vegas round. He took down ninth place for the year.

Buzz Calkins missed the Charlotte race due to injuries, placed fifth at Pike's Peak for his best result, still managed to round out the top 10.

While it had been expected the IRL's biggest challenge would be filling its fields, that turned out not to be the case. The number of starters ranged from 19 at the Disney World opener to 31 at the Las Vegas finale, with 35 at the league's crown jewel, the Indianapolis 500.

Veteran Robbie Buhl had a good, competitive campaign going until he crashed in practice at Pike's Peak, forcing him to miss that event and Charlotte, which followed. Back in harness for New Hampshire, he was a solid second to Eddie Cheever with three laps to go when Cheever's gearbox quit, handing him the victory.

The year's Cinderella story belonged to unsponsored rookie Jim Guthrie, whose team arrived at Phoenix with just enough financing for this event, which figured to be his last for a while. In storybook style, he outran favorite Tony Stewart over the last 10 laps, pocketed $206,453 in prize money, and signed sponsorship good for nearly $1 million. The rest of his year was less glamorous. It included a pair of crashes but finished on a high note with fourth place at Las Vegas and his being named Rookie of the Year.

Hard luck man of the year was Scott Sharp, the 1996 co-champion. He crashed at Indianapolis in practice, didn't get back into action until the Pike's Peak round. Having taken the pole, he spun on the first lap, incurring his second concussion of the campaign and was out for the season.

Accidents and the resultant serious injuries attributed to the lack of crushability in the back end of the new gearboxes took Davy Jones, Robbie Buhl, Mike Groff, and Scott Sharp out of action for at least one race each. An even larger number, Eliseo Salazar, John Paul Jr., Johnny O'Connell, and Jim Guthrie among them, incurred fractures. As the season progressed, the IRL instituted changes designed to reduce the injury level.

Despite its teething problems in 1997, the IRL appears to be on course in its goal of developing competitive open wheel racing on ovals, attracting new driving talent, some new spectators, and new sponsors. First time Texas had an estimated 128,000 attendance but second year New Hampshire and Las Vegas were down. There were two major off track happenings during the year. First, the dismissal of USAC as the IRL's sanctioning body after major officiating miscues; at Indianapolis (failure to fly the yellow flag following a late race accident) and at Texas (scoring Billy Boat as the winner when the victory really belonged to Luyendyk). Second, the appointment of highly respected motorsports veteran and ex-Goodyear racing chief Leo Mehl as Tony George's deputy.

For 1998, the series will be known as the Pep Boys Indy Racing League, signalling the signing on of a major title sponsor.

Cheryl Day Anderson

1 Setting the Standard for IRL... Tony Stewart had four pole positions in eight 1997 races, plus 812 laps in the lead (the second highest total was 122) attesting to his speed. Attesting to his paucity of racing luck was his lone victory. (278 IRL points)

Cheryl Day Anderson

2 Consistent Runner-Up... **Davey Hamilton** had no victories but seven top 10 finishes and only two DNFs which allowed him to come close. (272 IRL points)

Dan Bianchi

3 New Hampshire Polesitter... Marco Greco switched teams in mid-season. His best finish was fourth, but he still managed to tie for third in the points. (230 IRL points)

Dan Bianchi

4 Fast Starter... Eddie Cheever picked up the win in the 1997 opener at Disney World through another competitor's misfortune, lost the New Hampshire round through his own mechanical misfortune. (230 IRL points)

Cheryl Day Anderson

5 Another Near Miss... **Scott Goodyear**, for the second time in his career, had major misfortune, as a miscue cost him the victory in the rich Indianapolis 500. For the 1997 year he still had the highest points per race average. (226 IRL points)

6 Double Winner... Arie Luyendyk, a seasoned veteran, notched his second Indianapolis 500 win, added the Texas Indy Racing League inaugural to his win list. The rest of the year was marred by mechanical failure. (223 IRL points)

Cheryl Day Anderson

7 Best of the Nissan Contingent... **Roberto Guerrero** gave the Nissan engine its best ride of the year but even he switched to Aurora by the Pike's Peak round. (221 IRL points)

Dan Bianchi

8 No Repeat at Indianapolis... **Buddy Lazier**, the hero of the 1996 Indianapolis 500, gave it a good try in '97, but out of sequence pit stops dropped him to fourth. He consoled himself with the win at Charlotte's IRL debut. (209 IRL points)

Dan Bianchi

9 Big Comeback... **Eliseo Salazar**, a testing accident at Disney World kept him out of action for two events, but his persistence paid off with the win in the season ending Las Vegas round. (208 IRL points)

10 Tough Year... Buzz Calkins, the 1996 co-champion, was the victim of a test crash that kept him out of the Charlotte event, finished only two of the seven 1997 races he contested. Still made the top 10. (204 IRL points)

Dan Bianchi

Dan Bianchi

11 Impressive at Pike's Peak... Stephan Gregoire showed a high turn of speed on occasions. His runner-up finish at Pike's Peak was his best. (192 IRL points)

Dan Bianchi

12 Rookie of the Year... Jim Guthrie's almost unbelievable win at Phoenix on a fiscal shoestring was followed by bad luck the rest of the year, except for Las Vegas where he took a solid fourth place, (186 IRL points)

Dan Bianchi

Indy Racing League
Indy 200 at Walt Disney World
Presented by Aurora
January 25, 1997

EDDIE CHEEVER WINS AT LAST ON DISNEY WORLD OVAL

It wasn't the way he wanted it. Eddie Cheever's long-awaited first victory came with a red flag following three laps under caution. The winless veteran of scores of Formula One, CART, and now IRL races inherited his trip to victory circle when pole-sitter and race dominator Tony Stewart slipped on his own leaking oil, tagged the wall and handed the lead to Cheever. The ensuing yellow started on lap 146, lasted three laps, at which point the rains came in sufficient volume for USAC officials to call the race, thereby handing the win to Cheever. At that, Stewart had, himself, gotten the lead as a gift, when third fastest qualifier Buzz Calkins' engine blew up a few laps earlier. Second fastest qualifier Arie Luyendyk had already been eliminated in a crash resulting from Jeret Schroeder's spin. CART veteran Scott Goodyear put in a solid performance, qualifying sixth fastest and finishing third. Mike Groff, the top finisher powered by Infinity, took down second place with a conservative run that put him in the right place at the right time when the rains came. 1996 co-champion Scott Sharp qualified fourth fastest, finished in the same slot. Nine of the 19 starters finished and only one of the 10 non-finishers was listed as having engine failure. Oldsmobile and Aurora came out on top in the first race under IRL's new normally aspirated engine formula.

*The last two races of 1996 counted toward the 1997 championship in a year of transition to a calendar year championship, instead of one ending with the Indianapolis 500. They were covered in **Motorsports America, 1996-97**.*

Richard Dole

Jim Haines/IRL photo

Indy Racing League
Phoenix 200
at Phoenix International Raceway
March 23, 1997

CINDERELLA STORY AT PHOENIX. UNSPONSORED ROOKIE JIM GUTHRIE WINS

Running on fiscal fumes, unsponsored rookie Jim Guthrie arrived in Phoenix with one engine, a pick up crew, and just enough money to get through the weekend. Determined to make what could be his last race for a while, a good one, he qualified second fastest, right behind polesitter Tony Stewart, generally acknowledged to be the IRL's quickest driver. Stewart, as expected, took off in the lead, stayed there for the first 41 laps. Guthrie got a taste of the lead for a single lap, 42, liked it, re-took the lead from Stewart on lap 95, held on this time for 25 tours, before giving it back. On lap 154, rookie Guthrie swept around Stewart for the final time, running out the race with .854 seconds to spare over the polesitter. In between the Guthrie-Stewart pass and repass drama, Affonso Giaffone managed 13 laps in the lead, Kenny Brack, who crashed while leading, 24, and Scott Sharp, 4. Guthrie's victory was no fluke. Stewart had none of the mechanical problems that have plagued him previously. He simply came off second best to an inspired driver and his crew, which got Guthrie home on only two pit stops in a crash filled race. Having arrived in Phoenix with a second mortgage on his house, Guthrie left with a $170,000 purse, sponsorships in excess of $1 million, assured and highly improved prospects of making the field for the upcoming "big one," the Indianapolis 500.

Indy Racing League
81st Indianapolis 500
Indianapolis Motor Speedway
May 27, 1997

ARIE LUYENDYK OUTJUMPS TEAMMATE SCOTT GOODYEAR FOR HIS SECOND INDIANAPOLIS 500 VICTORY

Polesitter Arie Luyendyk responded quicker to the green flag at the start/finish line on the final lap more quickly than teammate Scott Goodyear alongside and earned his second big payday in the Indianapolis 500. Both were coming around turn four under the caution occasioned by debris from Tony Stewart's brush with the wall on lap 198. Both were expecting caution but Luyendyk capitalized on the green instantaneously and Goodyear was too late. Luyendyk was .570 seconds ahead at the checker in one of the more unusual finishes in the long history of the rich race. Luyendyk took down a $1,568,150 paycheck, more than $1 million richer than Goodyear's $513,300 payday. Stewart's mishap came as he attempted to get past sensational rookie Jeff Ward who was running third at the time. Ward finished third in his first Indianapolis 500, and might even have won with better pit timing. 1996 Indy 500 winner Buddy Lazier finished fourth, just ahead of Stewart. Ward actually led for 49 laps, while Stewart clocked the first 50 tours in front toward a total of 64 laps led, with winner Luyendyk close behind with 61. The top five finishers completed all 200 laps, and 14 cars were running at the finish, dispelling fears that the new normally aspirated engines were incapable of going 500 miles. A little known provision of the regulations allowed 35 starters, up from the traditional 33. After Sunday's race postponement, three of these were eliminated in a pace lap crash (Kenny Brack, Stephan Gregoire, and Affonso Giaffone) on Monday and two others (Sam Schmidt and Alessandro Zampedri) fell to mechanical failure before completing the first lap. After only a handful of laps, the race was again postponed. Run on Tuesday after the washouts on Sunday and Monday, the patient fans of the world's richest motor race were treated to some close and exciting competition.

Richard Dole

Linda McQueeney/IMS Photo

Indy Racing League
True Value 500
at Texas Motor Speedway
June 7, 1997

ARIE LUYENDYK WINS TWO IN A ROW IN CONTROVERSIAL TEXAS INAUGURAL

Tony Stewart was the polesitter again and again mechanical problems denied him the victory. Leading handily with two laps to go his engine let go. Billy Boat, in the Conseco G Force Aurora, driving for A.J. Foyt, sailed by and was ushered into victory circle. "Not so fast, we won," was the cry in Arie Luyendyk's camp, which filed an official protest. Most team scorers along pit road agreed with the Luyendyk version and so did USAC, the next day, moving Boat down to second place. By that time, however, Luyendyk had walked in on the Foyt camp's victory circle celebration and was punched and shoved by none other than Foyt himself. The contretemps earned both fines, Foyt's the larger. Davey Hamilton, in the A.J. Foyt G Force Aurora, earned the third finishing position, with Scott Goodyear, in the Treadway Nortel G Force Aurora, fourth. Tony Stewart, in the Glidden Menards Special G Force Aurora, salvaged fifth place, again another effort of winning caliber sacrificed to mechanical failure. While USAC admitted embarrassment for its miscue, the apology failed to salvage their tenure as the IRL's sanctioning body. IRL fired them and instituted its own scoring and timing team.

Richard Dole

Indy Racing League
Samsonite 200
at Pikes Peak
International Speedway
June 29, 1997

TONY STEWART FINALLY SHAKES HIS BAD LUCK, PREVAILS AT PIKES PEAK

This time Tony Stewart, in the Glidden/Menard's/Special G Force Aurora, didn't take the pole, but he was ahead where it counted, at the finish. He led all but seven of the 200 laps contested. Sensation of the race, Stephan Gregoire led five of those that didn't fall to Stewart and was putting the winner under the severe pressure at the end. So severe that Stewart's margin of vic-tory was a mere .222 seconds, the slimmest in IRL history. Davey Hamilton, in the A.J. Foyt Power Team G Force Aurora, nailed down third place from his fourth starting slot, getting around Eddie Cheever, in the FirstPlus G Force Aurora, at the end. Bad luck driver of the race was Scott Sharp, in the Conseco Dallara Aurora, just back from his Indianapolis practice crash. He qualified on the pole but crashed heavily on the first lap, probably ending his season. The accident list on the new circuit was long, including Robbie Groff, Kenny Brack, Arie Luyendyk, Jimmy Kite, and Johnny Unser. On the positive side, engine failure for the first time in '97 was nil.

Indy Racing League
Inaugural VisionAire 500
at Charlotte Motor Speedway
July 26, 1997

BUDDY LAZIER BLAZES THE WAY UNDER CHARLOTTE'S LIGHTS

Courageous Buddy Lazier, the 1996 Indianapolis 500 winner, who had been shut out of victory circle in 1997, found night racing to his liking. He shook off the challenge of rookie Billy Boat 10 laps from the end of the VisionAire 500 at Charlotte, and cruised to victory circle with a sizeable 3.301 second margin. Boat actually got by Lazier with 12 laps to go, but his tenure in front was short, only a single lap. Lazier had been held up by Scott Goodyear, trying hard not to be lapped. Lazier eventually managed the pass and Goodyear salvaged third place. Polesitter Tony Stewart put on another of his front running performances but had to give in to handling problems, finishing a lap down. Rookies Affonso Giaffone and Kenny Brack had their best finishes, fourth and fifth, two laps down. Another rookie, Jimmy Kite, in only his second Indy car race, actually led twice, only to find the wall on lap 164. Turnout for the event, deep in the heart of NASCAR territory, was excellent.

Richard Dole

Indy Racing League
Pennzoil 200
at New Hampshire
International Speedway
August 11, 1997

ROBBIE BUHL BESTS VINCENZO SOSPIRI IN CLOSE NEW HAMPSHIRE CONTEST

Back in harness after early season injuries, Robbie Buhl beat Vincenzo Sospiro to the wire in the Pennzoil 200 at New Hampshire by a scant .064 of a second, the closest margin of victory in the IRL's two year history. The driver who should have won, Eddie Cheever, wasn't even in the final run down. He had dominated the second half of the race, was leading comfortably with three laps to go, when his gearbox seized. Buhl, behind him, had to get on the brakes to avoid hitting Cheever's stricken racer. Buhl managed the maneuver successfully but lost momentum to a flying Vincenzo Sospiri, taking full advantage of the situation. Buhl was able to hold off Sospiri, but only barely. Arie Luyendyk, a front runner all day, netted third place. Polesitter Marco Greco, in the Monsoon Galles Racing G Force Aurora, led for the first 34 laps, dropped out with oil fitting problems. Second fastest qualifier Scott Goodyear was a strong factor, with two sessions in the lead, until sidelined by engine problems after 152 laps. A disappointed Cheever was now one for two in the luck department. He inherited the victory at the Disney World opener, had this one, which he had earned, snatched away just as summarily.

Indy Racing League
Las Vegas 500
at Las Vegas Motor Speedway
October 11, 1997

ELISEO SALAZAR'S COMEBACK TRAIL LEADS TO LAS VEGAS VICTORY

It was a long haul but worth the effort. Out of action from the time of his pre-season testing accident until the Indy 500, Eliseo Salazar persevered and was rewarded with his first IRL win at the challenging Las Vegas oval. Challenging indeed, the unseasonable temperatures were so low that officials ran the first three laps under caution. Billy Boat was on the pole with Davey Hamilton alongside. Points leader Tony Stewart started right behind this pair. The anticipated Stewart-Hamilton duel for the title never materialized. Up 10 points going in, Stewart ended up four laps down but with a six point margin over Hamilton, today's seventh place finisher. Stewart became the IRL's first full season driving champion and the first under the new chassis/engine formula. Polesitter Boat went out with electrical problems after 97 laps.

Jim Haines/IRL Photo

Indy car racing...   Las Vegas style

Richard Dole

When returning Barber Dodge veterans get their first look at the standard equipment for the 1998 season they are in for a major - and pleasant - surprise. First, there is an all new chassis, designed by the same Adrian Reynard whose Indy cars topped the win charts and produced the PPG Cup champions for the past two years. It's a scaled down version of the car used by more than three quarters of the teams on the '98 FedEx Championship circuit. The chassis incorporates a carbon composite monocoque, fitted with a 6-speed sequential gearbox. The standard engine continues to be Dodge's all aluminum V-6 rated at 250 horsepower, based on the engine available in the Dodge Intrepid. The racing engine is capable of further development, an option now that it is in a state-of-the-art chassis. The third new element in the equipment package consists of new standard tires, racing radials from Michelin, pioneers of the radial tire. When 1998 Barber Dodge competitors go after the more than $200,000 in prize money that '97 champion Derek Hill (and '96 champion Fredrik Larsson) won, they'll all be in the same state-of-the-art package, evenly matched. It's a series where driver skill, not bankroll counts. Speaking of bankrolls, prize money per race in '98 goes up to $55,000 from $40,000 and the year end "Career Enhancement Award" is doubled to $300,000.

NEW LOOK FOR BARBER DODGE IN 1998

Richard Dole

Pilot SX
ENGINEERED
Pilot
MICHELIN
TO • EXTREMES
MICHELIN

YUASA
PROGRESSIVE

A CHAMPION'S SON BECOMES A CHAMPION IN HIS OWN RIGHT

Derek Hill Prevails in a Tight Race for the Barber Dodge Title

Being the son of a racing champion, even a Formula One World Champion like Phil Hill, takes not a fraction of a second off the lap times of an aspiring young driver like Derek Hill, the 1997 Barber Dodge Champion. It does give him an insight into what's required to succeed in the highly competitive world of motorsports. The younger Hill combined his own rapidly developing talents, and some occasional fatherly advice, to prevail over a fast and eager field of young drivers, all in 250 horsepower Dodge-powered single-seaters owned, prepared, and maintained by Barber Racing. The Barber/Dodge format provides the "level playing field" that rewards driver ability, not the "cubic money" that often decides the winner in conventional series. Hill, the 1996 Rookie of the Year, had as his closest rival in a year long contest that wasn't decided until the 12th and final round at Laguna Seca, Italian Rino Mastronardi. Mastronardi actually won more races, five, than Hill who had four victories. He took the most poles, too, five versus Hill's three. Only in fastest race laps, three to Mastronardi's one did Hill outshine his rival in the statistical department.That, of course, doesn't take into account Hill's superiority in the points department, 157 versus 147, and the $150,000 in championship bonuses that went with Hill's title. Andy Boss, who gets his racing genes from 1950's sports car driving star, Russ Boss, checked in with a single victory and eight top five finishes for 135 points and third place in the standings. Chris Menninga scored a win, a pole, and a fast race lap for 130 points and fourth place on the board. Nicolas Rondet with 125 points, had a win, a pole and two fast race laps good for fifth place. His fifth place was also good for Rookie of the Year honors, giving him six "no charge" races for 1998 and a shot at the title. Rounding out the top six was Rocky Moran Jr., son of the Indy car driver, with 100 points, which included two fast race laps and three podium finishes. The talented teenager will be back in '98 and must be considered a serious candidate for championship honors. Martin Stenshorne exhibited considerable speed. His results were marred by an almost equal lack of patience. Add this element, and he could be a top contender with a lot more than his 67 points in 1997, seventh highest of this year. Will Langhorne expects to return in '98 and improve on his six top 10 finishes in 1997, good for 58 points and eighth place in the standings. Samer Hindi made the top five twice, scored 55 points as the ninth place driver.

1996 Co-Rookie of the Year Tony Renna showed considerable speed, as witness a pole position and two runner-up slots. A limited schedule held his point production down to 54 as the last driver in the year's top ten.

The year's big contest was the Hill/Mastronardi rivalry, in which Hill got off to a slow start with a DNF in the season's opener won by Mastronardi. Hill was 20 points behind the Italian going into the penultimate Reno round. He won after Boss shredded one of polesitter Mastronardi's valve stems, putting him out. The finale turned out to be less than climactic. The two points leaders were involved in a three car tangle with Martin Stenshorne on the first lap that put them both out of contention for the win, although Hill recovered to finish ninth. Hill nailed down the title and its big bonus without the down to the wire tussle with Mastronardi that both had been anticipating. The stewards ruled the tangle "a racing incident" and let the results stand. Mastronardi was understandably disappointed that racing luck had deserted his cockpit so precipitously at the end of a hard fought campaign that had exhibited so much promise.

Sidell Tilghman

1 Worthy Champion... Derek Hill, the 1996 Co-Rookie of the Year, made his sophomore season a winning one. (157 Barber Dodge points)

Sidell Tilghman

2 Unlucky at the End... Rino Mastronardi had the most victories, the most poles, and the title within reach, until racing luck deserted him in the last two rounds. (147 Barber Dodge points)

Sidell Tighman

3 Front Runner... Andy Boss was out of the top five only four times, scored his first victory. (135 Barber Dodge points)

Richard Dole

4 Quick Qualifier... Chris Menninga scored a single victory, a single pole, and missed the top 10 only on two outings. (130 Barber Dodge points)

Richard Dole

5 Rookie of the Year... Nicolas Rondet also scored a race win and a pole, should be a top contender for the title in 1998. (125 Barber Dodge points)

Richard Dole

6 Terrific Teen... Rocky Moran Jr. made the podium three times, another top contender for the '98 title. (100 Barber Dodge points)

Richard Dole

7 Often Up Front... Martin Stenshorne made the podium only once, but was a principal player in multiple up front battles. (67 Barber Dodge points)

Richard Dole

8 Developing Driver... Will Langhorne made six top 10 finishes, looks for improvement in '98. (58 Barber Dodge points)

Sidell Tilghman

9 Looking to '98... Samer Hindi scored a pair of top five finishes, shows potential. (55 Barber Dodge points)

Sidell Tilghman

10 Short Season... Tony Renna, 1996 Co-Rookie of the Year, missed four rounds but was twice the runner-up. (54 Barber Dodge points)

Barber Dodge Pro Series Race 1
Grand Prix of Florida
St. Petersburg, FL
February 23, 1997

RINO MASTRONARDI GOES WIRE-TO-WIRE IN ST. PETERSBURG SEASON OPENER

Polesitter Rino Mastronardi got himself outjumped at the start by 1996 co-rookies of the year Derek Hill and Tony Renna. But, by the end of the first lap, he was in command and never headed, enroute to victory circle. Hill and Renna banged wheels going into the first turn, putting Renna out and Hill back in the pack. Hill went out two laps later in a second tangle while striving mightily to get back up front. That left clear sailing to Mastronardi, who handled veteran G.J. Mennen Jr., the fourth fastest qualifier, and, the runner-up, with relative ease. Mennen staved off a charge from mid-pack starter Andy Boss who had to settle for third place. Puerto Rico's Victor Gonzalez posted the fastest race lap enroute to a fourth place finish. Italian Mastronardi was celebrating his first Barber Dodge victory after a "learning experience" 1996 season.

Barber Dodge Pro Series Race 2
12 Hours of Sebring
Presented by Chrysler
Sebring, FL
March, 15, 1997

DEREK HILL LEADS EVERY LAP AT SEBRING

Derek Hill and Tony Renna, the competitors who managed to take each other out on the first turn in the season opener, avoided that calamity at Sebring, although it was close. Hill, starting alongside polesitter Renna, managed to squeeze by Renna in the first turn and get clear. Renna was immediately engaged in a race long battle for second with St. Petersburg winner Rino Mastronardi, which involved a pair of passes and re-passes and let Hill concentrate on the road ahead. Renna won that dice and runner-up honors. Nick Rondet threatened the Renna-Mastronardi pair but not seriously enough to do more than settle for fourth place. Rocky Moran Jr., the 17 year old son of Indy car driver Rocky Moran, showed promise. He started back in the pack, moved up to fifth place at the end. He's yet another of the second generation drivers seeking experience and advancement in the series.

Sidell Tilghman

Barber Dodge Pro Series Race 3
Dixie Crystals Grand Prix
Savannah, GA
May 18, 1997

DEREK HILL GOES POLE-TO-POLE IN CLOSE SAVANNAH WIN

This time it was Derek Hill's turn to go pole-to-pole, in front on every lap of Savannah Harbor's picturesque street circuit. It was far from a runaway. Arch rival Rino Mastronardi was a mere .009 second behind at the finish in a race marked by not one but two red flags, which gave Mastronardi ample opportunity to put the pressure on Hill. Mastronardi's best shot came on the last lap of the race when Hill slid wide going into the next to last turn. He had enough momentum, however, to get across the finish line 18 inches ahead of his flying Italian rival. Seventeen year old Rocky Moran Jr. posted another fine drive to notch third place. Norway's Martin Stenshorne was the fourth place finisher. His countryman Jarle Gåsland qualified second fastest but got involved in a tangle with Andy Boss that took both of them out and initiated one of the red flags. The Hill/Mastronardi rivalry was now well and truly joined.

Geoffrey Hewitt

Barber Dodge's Skip Barber and Driver Coach Peter Argetsinger.

Barber Dodge Pro Series Race 4
Dodge Dealers at Lime Rock Park
Lakeville, CT
May 26, 1997

RINO MASTRONARDI GETS THE JUMP AT LIME ROCK, LEADS EVERY LAP

In the St. Petersburg season opener polesitter Rino Mastronardi got outjumped at the start. This time it was his turn to return the favor to polesitter Derek Hill. 27 laps of intense racing later Mastronardi was still in front. Not that Hill didn't try to get by. He did, but Mastronardi, aided by a tight circuit, was having none of it. Andy Boss made several tries at passing Hill. None succeeded and he had to settle for third place. Nick Rondet, the fourth fastest qualifier, finished in the same position. When Martin Stenshorne lost coolant on lap 13, Tony Renna, Jarle Gåsland, who had just set fastest race lap, and John McCaig went off the road in the ensuing skid. Chris Menninga managed to tip-toe through the unsettled situation, saved his car, fifth place, and some points that will be highly useful as the season wears on.

Richard Dole

Barber Dodge Pro Series Race 5
The Trans-Am at Mid-Ohio
Lexington, OH
June 15, 1997

DEREK HILL MASTERS MID-OHIO

Early season points leader Rino Mastronardi doesn't like Mid-Ohio's rolling road circuit. Points pursuer Derek Hill does. He was on the pole and led every lap from runner-up Tony Renna, the second fastest qualifier. Renna never got close enough to put a serious move on Hill. Indeed, Hill had actually put a lapped car between them when the race ended on yellow, due to a Joshua Rehm/Bill Tichenor encounter on lap 17 of the 20 scheduled. Third place Chris Menninga took a couple of looks at Renna but backed off. Despite his lack of affection for the circuit, Mastronardi qualified sixth and finished a respectable fourth, no real threat to the leaders. With the series moving to Watkins Glen and the halfway mark, Hill and Mastronardi have, between them, won every race, with Hill now trailing the Italian by a mere four points.

Barber Dodge Pro Series Race 6
Lysol 200
Watkins Glen, NY
June 29, 1997

RINO MASTRONARDI CAPTURES THE WATKINS GLEN INTERATIONAL

Polesitter Rino Mastronardi missed a shift at the start of the Watkins Glen International, allowing second fastest qualifier Chris Menninga to get around him in the first turn. Menninga's lead was short lived. A mere three laps into the contest, a chastened Mastronardi blasted by and was never seriously threatened. Derek Hill, setting the fastest race lap, got by Menninga with two laps to go to move into second place. Hill was shocked when Menninga turned the tables on the last lap to regain second place and runner-up honors. Tony Renna started third, finished fourth ahead of Norwegians Martin Stenshorne and Jarle Gåsland. Andy Boss became an airborne cropper while trying to wrest fifth place from the Norwegian pair plus Rocky Moran Jr. who were seriously competing for the spot. Mastronardi got another lesson in rolling starts, won anyway.

Sidell Tilghman

Barber Dodge Pro Series Race 7
Minnesota Grand Prix
Minneapolis, MN
July 6, 1997

NICK RONDET AVOIDS THE CRASH UP FRONT, CASHES IN AT MINNEAPOLIS

Nick Rondet got off to a bad start on the Minneapolis street circuit, happily for him. He was far enough behind not to be involved in a major first lap crash that knocked out or seriously delayed the leaders, close enough to take advantage and the lead. Polesitter Jarle Gåsland, second fastest qualifier Derek Hill, points leader Rino Mastronardi, Victor Gonzalez and Martin Stenshorne were the players in the big pileup. Gåsland, Gonzalez, and Stenshorne were knocked out of the race. Hill and Mastronardi were knocked off course. Hill recovered to rejoin the fray. Mastronardi abandoned his car until told by a marshall it was driveable. He remounted but was too far back to salvage even a few points. With Rondet running in the clear up front, for a 7.4 second margin of victory, Andy Boss picked up an uncontested runner-up slot. Mastronardi "teammate" Giovanni Gulinelli, for the first time, finished ahead of the team leader, taking third place. For Rondet, a bad start turned into a great finish.

Barber Dodge Pro Series Race 8
Miller 200 at Mid-Ohio
Lexington, OH
August 10, 1997

ANDY BOSS IN CHARGE AT MID-OHIO

If season long points leader Rino Mastronardi disliked the Mid-Ohio circuit in June he must have truly hated it in August. He was the loser in a wheel banging incident with Andy Boss that put him out of the race, out of the points, and cost him his series leadership. Equally galling was the fact that Boss survived the incident and went on to notch the win, his first ever in the Barber Dodge series. Boss dispatched polesitter Nick Rondet on the third lap and was never displaced from the lead, although Mastronardi tried mightily on the lap nine encounter that put the Italian on the sidelines. Nick Rondet, the polesitter, was cleanly passed by Boss on lap two, hung on for runner-up honors. Derek Hill, having qualified poorly for him, in sixth place, put his right foot down to take third place at the end. Third place pays 14 points, enough to earn him the series lead. Boss has been a consistent front runner, regularly threatening to crash the win column, but unable to nail down his initial victory until today. Happily, Rino won't have to face Mid-Ohio again in '97.

Richard Dole

Barber Dodge Pro Series Race 9
Texaco/Havoline 200
Elkhart Lake, WI
August 17, 1997

RINO MASTRONARDI RIDES HIGH IN ROAD AMERICA WIN

Polesitter Rino Mastronardi was passed not once but twice in the first lap by arch rival Derek Hill but was still on top at the end of the lap - and at the end of the race. Hill got by again on a lap eight restart to take the lead for a single circuit. On the next to last lap, Hill overcooked it, spinning into the gravel and handing the victory to Mastronardi. Running behind this pair, Andy Boss assumed second place with Hill's misfortune and applied the pressure to Mastronardi. Mastronardi failed to blink and ran out the last two laps .310 second ahead of runner-up Boss. Rocky Moran Jr. set the fastest race lap enroute to third place. From being down in second place, Mastronardi vaulted back into the series lead with a nine point cushion over Hill. Chris Menninga sprinted from a dead last starting slot to fourth at the finish. Hill and Mastronardi had been providing the fans with major excitement in their race long duel, until Hill made his mistake, one that would prove costly with only three races left.

Sidell Tilghman

Barber Dodge Pro Series Race 10
Grand Prix of Monterey
Monterey, CA
September 6, 1997

RINO MASTRONARDI PREVAILS AT LAGUNA SECA

Rino Mastronardi led the first three laps, when polesitter Chris Menninga put two wheels off just after the start. On lap three Derek Hill got past Mastronardi to lead the next six circuits, but his handling was deteriorating and Mastronardi cleanly re-passed on lap 11. Menninga, too, took advantage of Hill's handling problem and edged by for runner-up honors. Mastronardi now leads Hill by 15 points in the title chase, putting the American on the spot in the upcoming Reno round. Menninga, Boss and Rondet are still technically in the title tussle but the odds favor the two front runners. With arch rival Mastronardi now the clear possessor of the points lead and the momentum, Hill is facing a monumental task. His game plan is clear, beat Mastronardi. Mastronardi has the option of a more conservative approach, finish at all costs, giving away a few points as necessary, but don't get involved in any head-to-head encounters that could lead to an off-road excursion and no points at all. Whether Mastronardi has the temperament to adopt the less risky approach is questionable. He may try to wrap it all up at Reno. All it would take is a post race bulge of 21 points over Hill to clinch the title.

Barber Dodge Pro Series Race 11
Reno Grand Prix
Reno, NV
October 19, 1997

RENO RUN FALLS TO DEREK HILL

In the season's penultimate round at the Reno Hilton circuit, Rino Mastronardi seemed to have most, if not all, the chips; a 15 point lead over Derek Hill, and pole position. However, as it can in a gaming town, his luck soured. On the very first lap under green, Andy Boss, making a great start from the second row, clipped the tire stem on Mastronardi's right rear tire. Mastronardi, in time, had to stop for a replacement, finished out of the points. Boss took the lead and held it for three laps, at which point Derek Hill took over, rolling to a comfortable 1.650 second margin over runner-up Boss at the end. Martin Stenshorne, regularly a front runner, made the podium for the first time with his third place finish. From a 15 point deficit going in, Hill left Reno with a four point lead, enroute to the season finale at Laguna Seca. Mastronardi's options for the season's finale are now down to one; he must take the pole and win the race. Then the title becomes his even if Hill secures the runner-up position. Hill's slim four point lead is insufficient to leave him any room for relaxation, particularly if Mastronardi is successful in gaining the pole as he has been four times previously during the year. In short, Hill has to go for the win with the same urgency as Mastronardi.

Barber Dodge Pro Series Race 12
VISA Sports Car Championship
Monterey, CA
October 26, 1997

CHRIS MENNINGA LANDS THE VICTORY AT LAGUNA SECA. DEREK HILL CLAIMS THE CHAMPIONSHIP

The fans focused on the Derek Hill/Rino Mastronardi shoot-out for the Barber Dodge championship didn't have to wait long for action. Mastronardi had the pole, Hill was alongside on the front row. However, Martin Stenshorne stole the show by passing Mastronardi for the lead. Coming into turn five of the first lap Stenshorne led Mastronardi and Hill by the tiniest of margins. Stenshorne turned in, triggering a three car pile-up which sent all the participants into the gravel. Chris Menninga, starting in the third row, slipped through for a lead he would never relinquish. Hill got back on course to finish ninth. Mastronardi failed to complete a lap, finished dead last. Stenshorne struggled on for a few more laps and folded. Hill had his championship, albeit not the way he might have liked it. Mastronardi made a case with the stewards, who ruled the tangle a racing incident. Rocky Moran Jr. was the runner-up, followed by Nicolas Rondet. Hill was the first American Barber Dodge champion since Bryan Herta in 1991. Hill and Mastronardi hope to follow his steps up the racing ladder to success in the top level of American motorsports.

MUSTANG MAN TOMMY KENDALL
Runs Roughshod Over Trans-Am Field

No he wasn't perfect. In driving to his fourth Trans-Am title, Tommy Kendall allowed another Ford driver, and a rookie at that, to win the last two events of the 13 race 1997 Trans-Am Tour. The first eleven in a row were all Kendall's, setting a new record for Trans-Am, and likely for any major series. The rookie winner was Mike Borkowski, the Bobby Rahal protégé who put his Textron Mustang in front at the Pike's Peak and Reno rounds. With this pair shutting out the opposition, Ford wrapped up manufacturer's honors early. While Kendall dominated qualifying, he had to take whatever place on the starting grid, within the first five, called for by a numbered ball pulled out of a hat. This was Trans-Am's unusual practice of starting the five fastest qualifiers, labeled the "Goodyear Fast Five," by lot, presumably to make things more interesting up front.

Borkowski's two wins, both at the end of the year, weren't enough to earn him runner-up honors on the Tour. Those went to Brian Simo, whose pair of second place finishes at Phoenix and Road America, plus a high degree of consistency, earned him 277 points, the highest total after Kendall's 411. He was in contention for a win on two occasions, just didn't get the needed breaks. Borkowski was right behind Simo with the third highest total ot 275.

Voted the "Most Improved Driver" of the year, Jon Gooding also posted a pair of second place finishes, helping him to a season total of 272 points. He, too, displayed winning potential. Old Kendall foe Dorsey Schroeder was the only driver to qualify faster than the champion, which he did on two occasions. He also set fastest lap at two events. Despite these accomplishments, vic- tory did not beckon. His four second places were offset by three finishes below 20th place for a total of 265 points and fifth place on the Tour, well below his '96 runner-up finish. All of the top five drove Mustangs.

Head of the class among the Camaro standard bearers was sixth place Paul Gentilozzi. Admittedly, he and other Chevrolet drivers were without factory support, but in numbers they had a clear majority. A talented qualifier, he never failed to make the Goodyear Fast Five, but, on seven occasions, drew the unlucky number five starting slot. This meant starting on the third row. When he finished, he finished well, with a quartet of third places and fourth places, and actually improved on his 11th place in the '96 season standings.

Greg Pickett, the perennially competitive veteran Camaro driver, made the podium three times, including a fine second place at Detroit, where he started on the front row. He moved up one slot from his '96 ranking of eighth. 1996 Rookie of the Year, John Miller IV improved his standing in '97 taking eighth place in the year end totals. Pickett teammate Bill Saunders (they're the same age, 50) also moved up in the standings, despite missing the Mosport round, as did Pickett. His 168 points were good for ninth at season end. Mustang driver Michael Lewis rounded out the top 10. A pair of fourth places were the high points of his first season, in which he placed second to Bork-owski for Rookie of the Year honors. While they failed to make the top 10, rookie Peter Shea and part-timer Dino Crescentini are two, both Camaro exponents, who showed promise and are worthy of watching in 1998. Savvy veteran R.J. Valentine ran a reduced schedule, skipping three events, still managed a top 10 finish in half the races he entered.

During the year, Professional SportsCar's Andy Evans made a failed attempt to buy the Sports Car Club of America's professional racing division, with Trans-Am as its stellar attraction. This resulted in the formation by SCCA of an official Trans-Am council with respected Penske Racing executive and ex-NASCAR Vice President Les Richter at the head. This move served to quiet the turmoil. Then, in September, an announcement that a major Sears division, NTB, with B.F. Goodrich as exclusive tire supplier and marketing associate, would be the series sponsor in 1998 and beyond, augured well for the upcoming season.

The 1997 Trans-Am Tour will certainly go into history, with a collection of Tommy Kendall records, unlikely to be broken any time soon. A record that Tommy won't be breaking soon is that for total Trans-Am starts. As of year end, he had no ride for '98, since his Roush Racing Team had no Trans-Am plans for the new year.

Geoffrey Hewitt

Tommy Kendall took home the 1997 driver's championship with his record setting 11 consecutive Trans-Am victories.

Geoffrey Hewitt

1 Dominant Player... Tommy Kendall made the Trans-Am Tour his private highway with a record 11 straight Mustang-powered wins, showed he was human by dropping the last two races. (411 Trans-Am points)

2 "Most Determined"... Brian Simo showed grade A aggressiveness which brought him close to victory twice, earned him two runner-up finishes. (277 Trans-Am points)

Geoffrey Hewitt

3 Rookie of the Year... Mike Borkowski was the only driver to dent Kendall's winning ways which he did twice with victories at Pikes Peak and Reno. (275 Trans-Am points)

Dan Bianchi

4 "Most Improved"... Jon Gooding, Kendall's teammate, put his top drawer Roush Racing Mustang to good use, got the nod as the year's Most Improved Driver. (272 Trans-Am points)

Dan Bianchi

5 Fast Qualifier... Dorsey Schroeder was the only driver to qualify quicker than Kendall, which he did twice, was also one of only two outside of Kendall to set fastest race lap, but victory eluded the veteran. (265 Trans-Am points)

Dan Bianchi

6 Chevrolet Campaigner... Paul Gentilozzi qualified regularly in the top five, often hounded Kendall but could never get past him for a victory, despite setting fastest race lap at Phoenix. (265 Trans-Am points)

Dan Bianchi

7 Rapid Veteran... Greg Pickett retained top 10 status despite missing the Mosport round and nagging mechanical problems.
(228 Trans-Am points)

Dan Bianchi

8 Continued Progress... John W. Miller IV, the 1996 Rookie of the Year got better in 1997 with 10 top 10 finishes and a place in the year's elite top 10.
(195 Trans-Am points)

Dan Bianchi

9 Pickett Teammate... Bill Saunders suffered the same mechanical tribulations as his team leader, still managed to crack the top 10. (168 Trans-Am points)

Dan Bianchi

10 Promising Player... Michael Lewis displayed top 10 talent in his rookie year, along with promise that his sophomore season could be even better. (166 Trans-Am points)

Trans-Am Race 1
Kash n' Karry Florida Grand Prix
St. Petersburg, FL
February 23, 1997
60 Laps, 101.4 Miles

TOMMY KENDALL TAKES TOPSY TURVY ST. PETERSBURG OPENER

Some surprises are always to be expected in the first race of a new season, but the Trans-Am Tour's 1997 opener set a new high for upside down developments.

Tommy Kendall, the fastest qualifier in the All Sport Body Quencher Mustang, *did* win, followed by Roush Racing teammate Jon Gooding but not before Kendall had spun on Mike Lewis' transmission fluid on lap two. When his car wouldn't immediately start after the spin he was lucky to get back in action at the tail end of the lead lap. Leader Dorsey Schroeder, starting first under the new Trans-Am system of allocating the top five starting positions by lot to the five fastest qualifiers, broke a drive shaft relegating him to also ran status for the day. New leader Brian Simo was locked in a close contest with Paul Gentilozzi, which he lost for good when he had to pit to remove debris blocking his radiator. Meanwhile Kendall had been burning up the track and, with an assist from Gooding, got into second place. Kendall put the pressure on Gentilozzi, desperately trying to protect his lead. On lap 55, Gentilozzi wilted under pressure and made the small mistake that allowed Kendall and Gooding to get by for the win and runner-up honors. Gentilozzi salvaged third place.

Trans-Am Race 2
Phoenix International Raceway
Phoenix, AZ
April 19, 1997
67 Laps, 101.17 Miles

TOMMY KENDALL IN WIRE-TO-WIRE PHOENIX WIN

Tommy Kendall was the fastest qualifier at Phoenix. However, he got the pole position at the start by being lucky, and picking the no. 1 ball out of the hat from the five available to the five fastest qualifiers. Adding skill and speed to luck, he never allowed his All Sport Body Quencher Mustang to be headed. Brian Simo, in the Valvoline Ford Mustang, who started second, came closest. He piled on the pressure to no avail, was .680 second behind at the finish. On the first lap, Dorsey Schroeder, in the Raybestos Mustang, moved from his fourth starting position up to third, and that's where he finished. The race's biggest crowd pleaser was Paul Gentilozzi, in the RISO Chevrolet Camaro, who was making a charge on the leaders from seventh place when a distributor wire came loose. He repaired it on course, and went back to charging. It came loose again. Again, the errant wire responded to trackside repairs. This time Gentilozzi came into the pits for a new wire. Back out, he set the fastest race lap, finished in 14th place.

Trans-Am Race 3
Dodge Dealers Grand Prix
at Lime Rock Park
Lakeville, CT
May 26, 1997
66 Laps, 100.98 Miles

TOMMY KENDALL GOES THREE FOR THREE AT LIME ROCK

Tommy Kendall, again the fastest qualifier at 106.102 mph, started third under Trans-Am's lottery procedure but put his All Sport Body Quencher Ford Mustang out in front on lap one and every one of the 65 remaining in the Dodge Dealers Grand Prix at Lime Rock Park. A slight bobble by polesitter Greg Pickett, in the Autolink/Highway-Master Chevrolet Camaro, aided his cause. On lap 27, Dorsey Schroeder, holder of multiple Lime Rock wins, muscled by Pickett to launch his ardent race long pursuit of Kendall. Ardent, but unsuccessful, Schroeder, in the Raybestos Ford Mustang, was a full 1.362 seconds behind at the checker. Paul Gentilozzi, in the RISO Chevrolet Camaro, who started fifth, got past Brian Simo, in the Valvoline Mustang, who started on the front row to take third, in what was the day's best duel. Simo had to settle for fourth while polesitter Pickett was shuffled all the way back to ninth at the finish. Rookie Mike Borkowski, in the Textron Mustang, started sixth and finished in fifth place. The season is just started but already the big question in the paddock is, "Who will find the speed to handle Kendall?"

Geoffrey Hewitt

Trans-Am Race 4
Motor City 100
Belle Isle Park
Detroit, MI
June 7, 1997
48 Laps, 100.8 Miles

TOMMY KENDALL CRUISES TO VICTORY IN DETROIT'S MOTOR CITY 100

The Detroit round of the Trans-Am Tour attracts special attention just by reason of its site in the Motor City. Tommy Kendall made certain that, if anybody breaks his 1997 victory string, it won't be in Detroit. He started his All Sport Body Quencher Mustang on the pole and was never headed. Fellow front row starter Greg Pickett, in the Autolink/Highway Master Camaro, was a full 1.602 seconds behind at the end. Old Kendall rival Dorsey Schroeder, in the Raybestos Ford Mustang, crashed on lap 16 in his attempt to topple the flying Roush Racing pilot. Another old rival, Paul Gentilozzi, in the RISO Chevrolet Camaro, was sidelined after 41 laps with transmission trouble. Mike Borkowski, in the Textron Automotive Mustang, nudged Brian Simo, in the Valvoline Mustang, into a spin to take the final place on the podium, ahead of fourth finisher Jon Gooding, in the Mountain Dew Ford Mustang. With each race in the new season the Kendall legend grows, as does the incentive for other drivers to beat him to the checker.

Trans-Am Race 5
Mid-Ohio Sports Car Course
Lexington, OH
June 15, 1997
45 Laps, 101.25 Miles

TOMMY KENDALL MASTERS MID-OHIO

Tommy Kendall, in the All Sport Body Quencher Ford Mustang made it five in a row at Mid-Ohio, but Paul Gentilozzi started on the pole in his RISO Chevrolet Camaro and stayed out in front and in the clear for the first seven laps. At that point his engine called it a day. Kendall had earlier gotten around the other occupant of the front starting row, Dorsey Schroeder, who was having handling problems, and easily retained his lead until the end. Schroeder, in the Raybestos Ford Mustang, had to fight off long time Camaro driver Greg Pickett who was, on this occasion, driving a borrowed Roush Mustang and driving it well indeed. Pickett had crashed his own mount in practice. Despite being all over the course, Schroeder managed to hang on to runner-up honors, while Pickett, enjoying his rare Mustang ride, took down third. Mike Borkowski, in the Textron Automotive Ford Mustang, continuing to show signs of race winning potential, qualified fourth fastest, finished in the same slot. Michael Lewis, in the Redline Oil Mustang, started seventh finished in fifth place.

Trans-Am Race 6
Sprint PCS Grand Prix
Minneapolis, MN
July 6, 1997
63 Laps, 100.8 Miles

TOMMY KENDALL MAKES MINNEAPOLIS HIS SIXTH STRAIGHT VICTORY

Tommy Kendall and his All Sport Mustang kept their winning streak alive at six with a relatively easy victory in Minneapolis' Sprint PCS Grand Prix. Kendall, once again the fastest qualifier, started fifth under Trans-Am's lottery system but he was in front by lap eight. He had a little help from Brian Simo who started second. Simo nudged polesitter Paul Gentilozzi off the course and out of the lead on lap four. Simo was penalized and had to drop back behind Gentilozzi. This allowed a surging Kendall, followed by Dorsey Schroeder, who started third, into the lead. That order remained unchanged til the end with Kendall ahead by a comfortable 1.779 seconds. Gentilozzi, in a hurry to get back up front, made an additional off course excursion, ended up fourth, behind Jon Gooding, Kendall's teammate. If Kendall stays on course, he'll be in position to match or surpass Mark Donohue's record of eight consecutive wins in a single campaign. Kendall is also moving in on the $1 million mark in career Trans-Am earnings.

Trans-Am Race 7
Burke Lakefront Airport
Cleveland, OH
July 12, 1997
42 Laps, 99.54 Miles

TOMMY KENDALL GOES SEVEN FOR SEVEN AT CLEVELAND

Cleveland's wide straights and generous grassy run off areas make for some wild Trans-Am races, particularly in the early stages. The 1997 ediiton was no exception. Dorsey Schroeder, on the pole with teammate Brian Simo alongside were charging through turn one in close tandem when Paul Gentilozzi surged alongside Simo and turned him. This reversal of the Simo-Gentilozzi encounter of the previous race caused a five car encounter. This time Gentilozzi paid the penalty, forced back behind Simo, who had ended up near the back of the pack. On the ensuing lap five restart Kendall, now in second place, got a good jump on leader Schroeder and passed him. Schroeder refused to quit and made repeated exploratory runs on Kendall, none of them successful. Kendall prevailed by a margin of .719 second. With today's purse of $21,600 Kendall passed the $1 million mark in career Trans-Am earnings, setting a new record. His only disappointment was his broken streak of fastest qualifying runs. Schroeder was the spoiler here. Simo, in the Valvoline Ford Mustang, made a meteoric rise from 20th place on lap two to third at the end.

Trans-Am Race 8
Player's Grand Prix of Trois-Rivieres
Trois-Rivieres, Quebec, Canada
August 3, 1997
55 Laps, 82.83 Miles

TOMMY KENDALL ON TOP AT TROIS-RIVIERES

It took Tommy Kendall only three laps to get around polesitter Dorsey Schroeder at the Player's Grand Prix of Trois-Rivieres. The rest was cruise control all the way. Kendall's margin of victory over teammate Jon Gooding, in the Mountain Dew Ford Mustang, who finished second, was a huge 8.406 seconds. Schroeder faded to sixth at the end with a deflating tire. This time there was no contact between Paul Gentilozzi and Brian Simo. Gentilozzi, in the RISO Camaro, moved into a third place finish from his fifth starting slot. Simo, in the Valvoline Mustang, who started seventh, got by Gentilozzi cleanly in the early stages but lasted only 20 laps. A former Trans-Am standout, off the Tour to date in '97, Ron Fellows made a "guest appearance" in a Tom Gloy Mustang. Fellows qualified sixth fastest and set fastest race lap before leaving the contest with a blown engine. The victory was Kendall's eighth in a row, tying the record set by Mark Donohue in 1968, when Kendall's racing was confined to tricycles. Kendall was back in form in qualifying, too, taking his seventh pole of the year.

Trans-Am Race 9
The Serengeti Eyewear
Trans-Am Classic
Watkins Glen International
Watkins Glen, NY
August 9, 1997
42 Laps, 102.9 Miles

TOMMY KENDALL BREAKS THE RECORD FOR CONSECUTIVE WINS

Watkins Glen was the scene of Tommy Kendall's record breaking ninth consecutive single season Trans-Am victory. The seemingly unstoppable All Sport Ford Mustang driver went into the record books in style. He was the fastest qualifier, started on the pole, and never looked back on his way to victory circle. Paul Gentilozzi drove a strong race in his RISO Chevrolet Camaro, passing Dorsey Schroeder on the last lap, to take runner-up honors. Neither Schroeder nor Gentilozzi was ever close enough to put any meaningful pressure on Kendall, despite four restarts due to the numerous crashes back in the pack. Kendall was .985 seconds ahead at the finish. More than half the laps were run under caution, leading to the relatively low average speed of 71.475 mph. Schroeder salvaged third place at the finish over Jon Gooding, Kendall's teammate. Indy car driver Alessandro Zampedri, seriously injured in the 1995 Indianapolis 500, made his Trans-Am debut in the Dinema Chevrolet Camaro, finishing a respectable seventh.

Trans-Am Race 10
Texaco/Havoline 200
at Road America
Elkhart Lake, WI
August 16, 1997
25 Laps, 100 Miles

TOMMY KENDALL TAKES HIS 10th STRAIGHT WIN AT ROAD AMERICA

Not only did Tommy Kendall take his 10th straight win at Road America, he nailed down the Trans-Am Tour driver's championship, his third in a row. The Mustang driver was also the major contributor to Ford's manufacturer's championship notched previously. For the second time this year Dorsey Schroeder, in the Raybestos Ford, out-qualified Kendall. He started on the pole on a wet but drying track, but failed to hold off Kendall for even a single lap. On lap 11 Brian Simo and Paul Gentilozzi did a replay of their bumping act and both went off course, without noticeable damage. On the restart Schroeder went off into the gravel trying to keep up with the flying Kendall. On lap 20 Kendall decided that the drying circuit called for a tire change and pitted. This let Simo, who stayed out, into the lead for three laps. He fell to a flying Kendall on the next to last lap but managed to hold off Gentilozzi and claim runner-up honors. Wet or dry, Kendall's superiority seemed clear. He posted a huge 25.531 second margin of victory over Simo.

Trans-Am Race 11
Mosport Park 500
Bowmanville, Ontario, Canada
August 31, 1997
40 Laps, 98.36 Miles

TOMMY KENDALL RAISES THE RECORD TO 11 STRAIGHT AT MOSPORT

Tommy Kendall was Mosport's fastest qualifier but started fifth in Trans-Am's lottery system for the fastest five qualifiers. The surprise polesitter was Indy car driver Alessandro Zampedri, the fifth fastest qualifier in only his second Trans-Am outing. Zampedri, in the Dinema Camaro, who lasted only three laps in front on a damp track before falling to Kendall, crashed out of competition after 23 tours. On lap 13, with the track drying, Kendall pitted allowing Jon Gooding, in the Mountain Dew Mustang, and Max Lagod, in the Hypermax Engineering Camaro, to claim a lead lap. Back on the track it was all Kendall again. He had a 1.373 second margin over runner-up Dorsey Schroeder in the Raybestos Mustang. Jon Gooding shrugged off a tap from Brian Simo to retain third place at the end. With his 11th straight victory, Kendall erased two more Trans-Am records: Most consecutive wins over two seasons, Bob Tullius (1978-79) and most wins in one season, Mark Donohue (1968).

Trans-Am Race 12
Pikes Peak International Raceway
Fountain, CO
September 27, 1997
73 Laps, 97.82 Miles

TOMMY KENDALL'S WIN STREAK BROKEN. MIKE BORKOWSKI PREVAILS AT PIKES PEAK

It took two spin inducing taps from behind to do it, but Tommy Kendall was finally foiled in his campaign to win every race on the 1997 Trans-Am Tour. Not by one of his old rivals, Paul Gentilozzi or Dorsey Schroeder, but by a rookie, Mike Borkowski, in the Textron Mustang. Borkowski, not satisfied with his Rookie of the Year title earned in the previous race, started on the pole, the beneficiary of the Trans-Am's "Fast Five" draw for the first five starting slots. Kendall, the fastest qualifier, ended up in the fifth starting position. On the first lap Schroeder tagged Kendall sending him all the way back to 17th, while Borkowski made a great start and went flying off into the lead. Schroeder meanwhile took off after leader Borkowski and was poised to pass when a blown tire knocked him out of contention. A determined Kendall muscled his way back into second place and repeatedly nudged Borkowski to let him know that he wanted to get by. Borkowski would have none of it. On the last lap Kendall got into position to "go for it" and edged Borkowski neatly out into the grass. The rookie got back on the course, bumped Kendall into a spin and ran out the race in the lead. Greg Pickett got by eternally dueling Brian Simo and Paul Gentilozzi to claim third place. Some observers felt that SCCA officials would penalize Borkowski. They didn't and Kendall's consecutive win mark was halted at 11, a record that will be hard to beat.

Trans-Am Race 13
Reno Hilton Street Circuit
Reno, NV
October 19, 1997
75 Laps, 95.25 Miles

MIKE BORKOWSKI NOTCHES TWO IN A ROW IN RENO FINALE

Already the 1997 champion, Tommy Kendall had a score to settle in the Trans-Am Tour finale at Reno... beat Mike Borkowski, the rookie who broke Kendall's winning streak at 11, in the previous Pikes Peak round. It may take a while for Kendall to get even. Although he was the fastest qualifier, he started fourth, never led a lap and finished 11 laps down in 17th place after his power steering failed. A time consuming pit stop failed to correct the malady. To top things off, Borkowski was the winner. He led only three laps, the last three. Paul Gentilozzi, the polesitter, and the leader of the first 39 tours and Brian Simo, in front for the next 32 laps, had a race long hammer and tongs battle. It ended on a lap 73 restart when they took each other out. Gentilozzi somehow managed to limp home in his battered Camaro for fourth place. Simo's Mustang was finished. He was scored in ninth place. Avoiding this contretemps, Mustang-mounted Borkowski collected the win. Max Legod slipped his Camaro into second place and Leighton Reese brought his Pontiac Grand Prix home in third, the season's best placing for both. Dorsey Schroeder, who started second, could have been a factor but was bumped out of contention early in the race by Gentilozzi.

BUTCH LEITZINGER IN ROB DYSON'S R&S FORD TAKES THE WORLD SPORTSCAR TITLE

A Year of Great Racing Tinged by Political Turmoil

1997 Champion Butch Leitzinger, Elliott Forbes-Robinson, and James Weaver, the top three finishers in SportsCars' Exxon World Sports Car series, didn't pay too much attention to the political clouds swirling around the series. They just drove their Rob Dyson owned R&S Fords - and extremely well at that. For the entrants, it was a different story. SportsCar, which used to be IMSA, had at its top, the colorful Andy Evans, who also drove for one of the top Ferrari teams, which he also owned. That is he drove in the year's two big events, the Rolex 24 at Daytona and the Superflo 12 Hours of Sebring. At Sebring, SportsCar officials were accused by the Dyson team, entrants of the Daytona winning Rain-X R&S Ford, of a faulty yellow flag/pace car procedure that allowed the Evans Ferrari to gain an extra lap. The procedure was corrected but no penalty was assessed. After Sebring, Evans stepped down as entrant and driver to concentrate on the sanctioning side. He offered to buy the SCCA's Pro Racing Division, an offer that was not only rebuffed, but led to the formation by SCCA of a revived U.S. Road Racing Championship to compete directly in Evans' arena. USRRC quickly gained sanctioning rights for the 1998 Rolex 24 at Daytona and the First Union six hour round at Watkins Glen, also owned by ISC, Daytona's parent company. By year end Evans had sold his Professional SportsCar Racing sanctioning group to a group including some former employees, seemingly in a holding operation for eventual sale to a larger, better financed group. One such group, Interpublic, a major advertising agency holding company, entered into negotiations via one of its subsidiaries, with Les Delano, an experienced marketing executive and endurance racing driver as its point man. As of year end the sale had not been consummated. Enter a new major player, Donald Panoz, the highly successful businessman who owns Panoz Auto Development, producer of the Panoz GTR-1, a sensation on the international and North American GT circuits in 1997. He owns a handsomely refurbished Road Atlanta, a regular venue for SportsCar events, and bought the Sebring lease from Evans. His weight could be an important factor in swinging any sanctioning body.

It seems reasonable to state that all the key car owners want is a viable series and a recognized championship. Despite all the confusion, it appeared from advance reports that the 1998 Rolex 24 at Daytona would attract a record number of entries and a record crowd.

All the rumbling on the political horizon, couldn't obscure the fact that the 1997 Professional Sports Car Racing series produced some of the most colorful, competitive and exciting prototype and GT racing seen in North America in years.

Starting with the Rolex 24 at Daytona where the smoking but circulating Rain-X R&S Ford, with Butch Leitzinger at the helm, managed to hang on and win over the rapidly gaining Evans/Velez Ferrari 333SP, down to the final round at Laguna Seca, also won by Leitzinger, the racing was close and fan pleasing. Leitzinger scored five wins, Weaver four, and Forbes-Robinson one. As usual, their main opposition came from the Ferrari 333SPs. Italian Andrea Montermini, partnered by Brazilian Antonio Hermann in Hermann's 333SP was extremely fast, but missed two races and ended up sixth in the points behind Hermann. They teamed for three wins. In his first year as a Ferrari driver, young Rob Morgan scored a single win and took down fourth place in the points chase. Two-time champion Wayne Taylor, along with partner Eric van de Poele, R&S Olds-mounted, had a dismal, for them, season. No wins, after Taylor scored four victories in '96, led to seventh and eighth in the points. The top 10 was rounded out by Jim Pace (R&S Olds) and veteran Jim Downing in his Kudzu Mazda. John Paul Jr. missed four events due to his IRL commitments, barely missed the top 10, but contributed substantially to driving partner Leitzinger's success, as he did to Ford's manufacturer's success. The talk of the GTS-1 series was the Panoz of Andy Wallace and Doc Bundy, which won three of the first five events. No they didn't take the title; Andy Pilgrim often co-driving with Allan McNish in Rohr Motorsports' new Porsche GT1, did that, but they made it very interesting. Bundy notched second place in the season standings ahead of third place Roger Schramm. Had the Panoz been around for Daytona, it might have been a different story. In GTS-2 the battle between a pair of Porsche drivers went down to the wire, with Larry Schumacher getting the nod over Franz Conrad. Martin Snow took down third place. For GTS-3 it was a repeat of 1996's BMW manufacturer's title. The championship went to BMW driver Bill Auberlen, followed by teammate Javier Quiros and Porsche driver David Murry.

1997 SportsCar WSC Manufacturers' Points

1.	FORD, 264 points
2.	FERRARI, 258 points
3.	OLDSMOBILE, 209 points
4.	MAZDA, 143 points
5.	BMW, 56 points

1 Top Driver on a Star-Studded Dyson Team... Butch Leitzinger posted five victories enroute to the World SportsCar championship. (231 WSC points)

Rick Dole

2 Early Points Leader... Elliott Forbes-Robinson made the grade as a full time member of the Dyson team. (213 WSC points)

Shelly Schmidt

3 Perennial Fan Favorite... James Weaver scored four victories. (212 WSC points)

Geoffrey Hewitt

4 First Year Ferrari Driver... Rob Morgan rode into the WSC victory circle for the first time. (189 WSC points)

Shelly Schmidt

5 Businessman Ferrari Driver... Antonio Hermann managed to get away from the office for three victories. (176 WSC points)

Geoffrey Hewitt

6 Come From Behind King... **Andrea Montermini** thrilled the crowds with his all-out charges, which garnered him three victories. (175 WSC points)

Shelly Schmidt

7 Shut Out in '97... **Wayne Taylor**, winner of four races and his second title in '96, won none in '97, largely due to mechanical problems. (164 WSC points)

Geoffrey Hewitt

9 Repeat Top Tenner... Jim Pace made the grade with a new team. (148 WSC points)

Shelly Schmidt

8 Taylor Co-Driver... Eric van de Poele was fast and consistent, couldn't overcome the team's mechanical difficulties. (163 WSC points)

Geoffrey Hewitt

10 Perennial Privateer... Jim Downing cracked the top 10 with cars of his own design. (141 WSC points)

Shelly Schmidt

GTS-2 Repeat Winner... Larry Schumacher, a devoted Porsche enthusiast, took his '97 title in a close race decided by the slim margin of three points. (246 points)

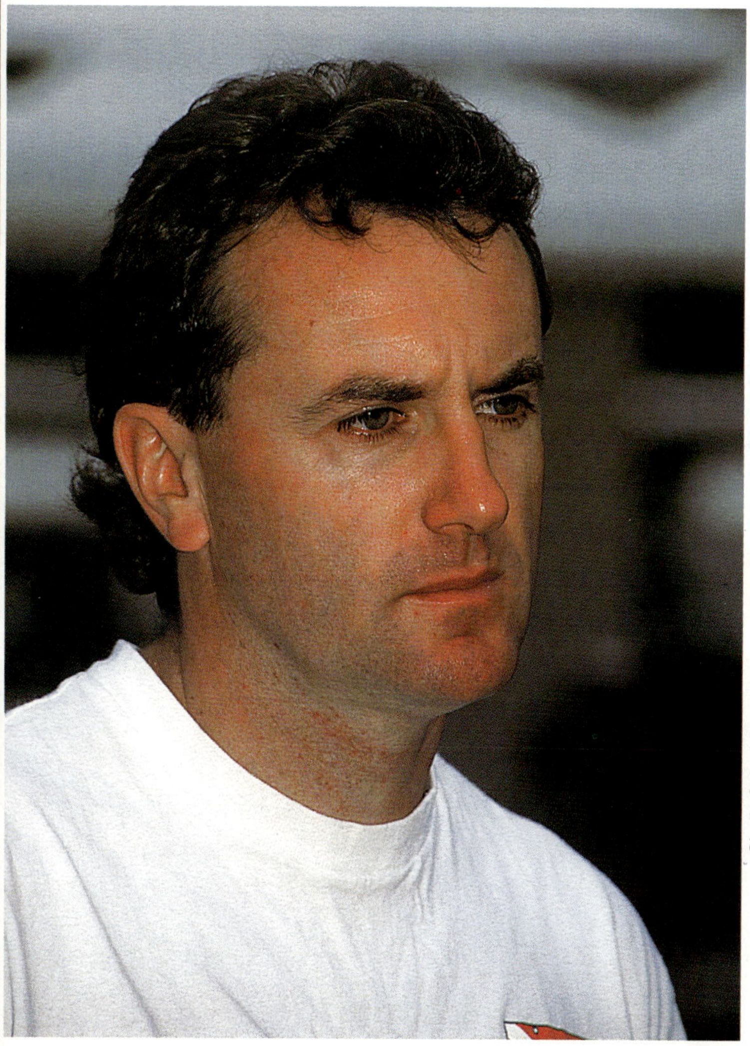

Shelly Schmidt

GTS-1 Porsche Protagonist... Andy Pilgrim drove the new Porsche GT1 to a string of four victories in the second half of the campaign and the title. (231 points)

Shelly Schmidt

GTS-3 BMW's Pointman... Bill Auberlen headed a potent BMW team, defeated a teammate for the year's GTS-3 honors. (234 points)

Shelly Schmidt

DRAMA AT DAYTONA, DYSON RACING'S R&S FORD CAPTURES THE ROLEX 24

Exxon World SportsCar/Exxon Supreme GT Presented by Virgin Interactive Championship Race 1
Rolex 24 at Daytona
Daytona Beach, FL
February 1 - 2, 1997
3.56 Mile Road/Oval Course

The finish of 24 hour endurance races often lacks electricity... Not the 1997 edition of the Rolex 24 at Daytona. For the final 20 minutes, the record crowd was on its feet as a drama was played out between the Rain-X R&S Ford driven by Butch Leitzinger, visibly smoking but still circulating in the lead, and the fast closing Scandia Ferrari driven by Fermin Velez, the quickest qualifier. The wounded Ford, with a two lap margin, was a candidate to expire at any moment; the Ferrari sounded and performed like it was fresh off the trailer. Despite making up huge hunks of time on every lap, the Ferrari 333SP couldn't catch the Ford that threatened to blow - but didn't. Instead the Dyson entered R&S Ford and its driving team were ushered into victory circle to receive the trophy from Rolex Watch USA President Roland Puton. The drama had started with a two lap cushion for the Ford. It ended with a winning margin of a little over a lap. The winning car had no less than seven drivers, including team owner Rob Dyson. The team of John Paul Jr., Andy Wallace, James Weaver, and

Richard Dole

The winning Rain-X R&S Ford required extra ministrations of oil and water to keep it running in the last 20 minutes as it fended off the fast closing Scandia Ferrari 333SP.

Leitzinger who put the faster Dyson R&S no. 16 into the lead, switched to the slower no. 20 car when theirs expired at the eight hour mark. Following the Scandia Ferrari home was another R&S, this one Olds-powered, driven by Eduardo Dibos, Jim Pace, and Barry Waddell. Surprisingly the next place, fourth overall, went to a GTS-2 Porsche with drivers Ralf Kelleners, Patrice Groueslard, Andre Ahrle, and Claudia Huertgen, followed by the GTS-1 Porsche of Andy Pilgrim, Harald Grohs, Arnd Meier, and Jochen Rohr. Sixth overall was another GTS-1 Porsche with Hans Stuck, Thierry Boutsen, and Bill Adam. The second best Ferrari was the seventh place Gianpiero Moretti entry. Eighth overall went to another GTS-2 Porsche with a European American driving team. The top GTS-3 car, a BMW M3, rolled home in ninth place overall with a driving team led by Bill Auberlen and including Derek Hill and Boris Said. A crowd pleasing Dodge Viper was the third place GTS-1 car in the hands of a team composed of Olivier Beretta, Dominique Dupuy, and Tommy Archer, but it was not among the first 10 finishers. Although Scandia team owner Andy Evans had to settle for second place in the 24 hour contest, he could console himself with the record entry (80 qualified for the race including 16 WSC cars) and a record crowd.

Geoffrey Hewitt

Exxon World SportsCar/
Exxon Supreme GT
Presented by Virgin Interactive
Championship Race 2
Superflo 12 Hours Presented by
Chrysler Corporation
Sebring International Raceway
Sebring, FL
March 15, 1997
3.6 Mile Road Course

SCANDIA FERRARI FIRST AT SEBRING 12 HOURS

Andy Evans' Scandia Ferrari, driven by himself, Fermin Velez, Yannick Dalmas, and Stefan Johansson narrowly turned the tables on the Daytona winning Dyson team of James Weaver, Butch Leitzinger, Andy Wallace, and John Paul Jr. in the Superflo 12 Hours of Sebring. Not, however, without a controversial yellow flag-pace car incident which allowed the Scandia driver to gain a lap advantage. Apparently the pace car failed to pick up leader Dalmas as prescribed. Protests by the then second place Dyson team in the Rain-X R&S Ford and the third place Moretti team in their Ferrari 333SP were answered by allowing them around the pace car. However, no penalty was assessed to Dalmas. After a race long duel between the Scandia Ferrari and the Dyson Ford, marked by eight lead changes, the red Italian car with 12 cylinders and 4 camshafts prevailed over the white 8 cylinder American vehicle by 47.465 seconds, a small margin in a 12 hour endurance contest. Eduardo Dibos, Jim Pace, and Barry Waddell, in the Dibos Ferrari 333SP, took down third place, 13 laps behind the two leaders. Fourth place went to Jim Downing's Mazda Kudzu, while fifth went to the second Dyson entry.

The GTS-1 winner was the surprising Irv Hoerr Olds Aurora, sixth overall ahead of the first Porsche, Jochen Rohr's 911, which placed seventh overall. GTS-2 went to a Porsche team headed by Bob Wollek in eighth overall. Bill Auberlen headed the BMW M3 team that claimed ninth overall, first in the GTS-3 class. Last of the top 10 finishers was the GTS-2 Porsche driven by Michel Ligonnet of France, Claudia Hurtgen of Germany, and a pair of Americans, Zack Brown and Dirk Layer.

If the results of the new year's first two events are indicative, the season will be marked by pitched battles between the Dyson Fords and which ever Ferrari is fastest on any particular day.

Exxon World SportsCar/
Exxon Supreme GT
Presented by Virgin Interactive
Championship Race 3
NAPA Auto Parts
Grand Prix of Atlanta
Road Atlanta
Braselton, GA
April 20, 1997
2.52 Mile Road Course

DYSON R&S FORDS DOMINATE ROAD ATLANTA

Ferraris qualified by Fermin Velez and Andrea Montermini were on the front row at the start of the NAPA Grand Prix of Atlanta. By the time the first lap was completed they were behind Butch Leitzinger in one of the Rob Dyson R&S Fords. Partnered by James Weaver, Leitzinger was out of the lead only for three laps when his teammate Elliott Forbes-Robinson, in the second Dyson R&S Ford, took over and four that went to Montermini on a pit stop shuffle. Leitzinger finished a relaxed 5.128 seconds ahead of Forbes-Robinson. Montermini ended up a lap down and polesitter Velez was down six laps when the Ferrari 333SP stalled late in the race with teammate Eduardo Dibos at the helm.

In the separate race for GT cars, the Panoz GTR-1 handled by Doc Bundy and Andy Wallace for its manufacturer, Donald Panoz, was the class of the field, piling up a huge 21.830 second margin of victory in taking first overall and GTS-1 honors. Stu Hayner, who put his surprising Camaro on the pole, was runner-up overall and in GTS-1. Third overall went to the GTS-2 Porsche driven by Larry Schumacher and John O'Steen, which took class honors. Porsche pilots Jim Matthews and David Murry took eighth overall and the GTS-3 win. The normally very competitive BMW M3s had a bad day at the office. Derek Hill crashed on the first lap, Bill Auberlen went out with a broken drive shaft, and Dieter Quester got shuffled out of the lead pack into fifth place in GTS-3.

Exxon World SportsCar/
Exxon Supreme GT
Presented by Virgin Interactive
Championship Race 4
Connecticut Lottery Presents the
Dodge Dealers Grand Prix
Lime Rock Park
Lakeville, CT
May 26, 1997
1.54 Mile Road Circuit

MOMO FERRARI ON TOP AT LIME ROCK FOR THE FOURTH STRAIGHT YEAR

The Momo Ferrari team loves Skip Barber's beautiful Lime Rock layout. They should, since they've won every WSC race there over the four year period starting in 1994, when they got their first Ferrari 333SP. This time the drivers were Antonio Hermann and Andrea Montermini and their chances looked slim for the first 53 laps. Polesitter James Weaver, in Rob Dyson's R&S Ford, had built up a lap lead over the closest Ferrari before turning over the car to teammate Butch Leitzinger. Leitzinger soon encountered electrical problems, and was forced to pit. Incredibly, Andy Wallace, in the second Dyson R&S Ford, had a fire under the dash, was forced to pit at the same time. This dual disaster handed Montermini his lap back, and the lead, which he relinquished only for four laps on a pit stop, to Bill Auberlen, in another Ferrari 333SP. After repairs both Dyson cars tried mightily to catch Montermini but failed. The Wallace/Forbes-Robinson car ended up second, 20.753 seconds off the pace. Leitzinger salvaged fifth place, two laps down. Jim Pace's Olds-powered R&S nailed down third place after a last lap tangle with Auberlen's Ferrari. Auberlen went over the finish line backwards to hold on to the fourth finishing slot.

In the separate GT race, Stu Hayner put his Camaro on the pole and into victory lane for overall and GTS-1 honors. Second overall and first in GTS-2 went to the Larry Schumacher, John O'Steen Porsche. Next in line at the finish in a remarkable performance were three GTS-3 BMW M3s piloted by Javier Quiros-Derek Hill-Dieter Quester-Marc Duez, and Boris Said-Bill Auberlen. The Panoz GTR-1 driven by Paul Newman and Doc Bundy created quite a stir, leading for 13 laps before falling back to seventh overall, second in GTS-1.

Exxon World SportsCar/
Exxon Supreme GT
Presented by Virgin Interactive
Championship Race 5
First Union Six Hours at the Glen
Watkins Glen International Raceway
Watkins Glen, NY
June 1, 1997
3.4 Mile Road Course

RAIN & MULTIPLE CRASHES CAN'T STOP THE DYSON R&S FORD AT WATKINS GLEN

Britisher James Weaver is one of the premier rain drivers on the World SportsCar circuit, or, indeed, any other circuit. His skills, and those of teammates Butch Leitzinger and Elliott Forbes-Robinson were key to the runaway success of the Dyson R&S Ford in Watkins Glen's rain slicked six hours. Quite a few of the competitors, including polesitter Andrea Montermini, in the Moretti Ferrari 333SP, went off course. Montermini was leading on lap 111 when he made his spectacular exit, handing the point position to Weaver. Montermini was the only real threat to the Dyson drivers, although Wayne Taylor somehow managed to get on the lead lap after being four laps down. He exited with a burnt piston. Rob Morgan and Eliseo Salazar, in the Morgan Ferrari 333SP, ran a relatively conservative race, stayed on course, and were rewarded with runner-up honors. Doc Bundy, Andy Wallace, and David Brabham had a spectacular run in the Panoz GTR-1 taking down third place overall and first in GTS-1. John Morton and Pete Halsmer, in the Mattco BMW M3, beat all the GTS-2 cars with their seventh place overall finish, good for a class first. Nick Ham, Franz Conrad, and Michel Lignonnet, in ninth place overall, were the GTS-2 winners over a small field. Weaver and company had a one minute 20 second edge at the end.

Exxon World SportsCar/
Exxon Supreme GT
Presented by Virgin Interactive
Championship Race 6
Toshiba Copiers & Fax
California Grand Prix
Sears Point Raceway
Sonoma, CA
July 13, 1997
2.52 Mile Road Course

DYSON DOES IT AGAIN, R&S FORDS ONE-TWO AT SEARS POINT

James Weaver and Andy Wallace won an intramural battle with Dyson Racing teammates Elliott Forbes-Robinson and Butch Leitzinger to take Sears Point's Toshiba Grand Prix. Weaver and Wallace did it the hard way, too, starting 16th as penalty for changing the engine in their R&S Ford after qualifying third fastest. Their task was eased when Antonio Hermann went seriously off course in the Ferrari 333SP which teammate Andrea Montermini had qualified on the pole. The excursion started a small grass fire and ended the Ferrari's day. The Eduardo Dibos Ferrari 333SP, which had been qualified by partner Fermin Velez on the front row, led laps 33 and 34 on pit stops by the two leaders. After that it was all Dyson with the Weaver-Wallace pair running out the last 11 laps to win with a 9.432 second lead.

The separate GT race was another patented Panoz production. Drivers Andy Wallace and Doc Bundy put the GTR-1 on the pole and led all but laps 32 to 45 of the 59 contested. Second overall and second in GTS-1 was the Camaro of Roger Schramm and Stu Hayner. Bill Auberlen and Boris Said gave their BMW M3 a great ride for third place overall, first in GTS-3. Frank Konrad-Nick Ham placed fourth overall, topped the GTS-2 class.

Exxon World SportsCar/
Exxon Supreme GT
Presented by Virgin Interactive
Championship Race 7
Mosport Festival
Mosport Park
Bowmanville, Ontario, Canada
August 25, 1997
2.459 Mile Road Course

OLD CANADIAN HAND RON FELLOWS THE KEY TO ROB MORGAN'S FIRST WSC VICTORY AT MOSPORT

Trans-Am standout Ron Fellows had never seen the cockpit of a Ferrari 333SP before the weekend, but, as a top Canadian driver, he had seen a lot of the Mosport track. Rob Morgan pulled a coup when he hired Fellows, who had no regular '97 ride, to co-drive his 333SP at Mosport. Fellows took instantly to the 333SP, putting it on the pole and leading the first 30 laps. When Morgan got in the car, he slipped down the standings, but maintained his position with the lead pack. Fermin Velez, in the Dibos Ferrari, asserted his strength on lap 60, taking over the lead from Wayne Taylor in the R&S Olds, who pitted for additional oil. Morgan and James Weaver, the Dyson standard bearer, in the R&S Ford were next in line. Velez, pulling away from his pursuers, appeared to have the race in hand. However, he had a problem, fuel was running low. Despite slowing to conserve his precious supply, Velez ran out with two laps to go. Morgan did an excellent job of holding off the more experienced Weaver and notched his first WSC victory, albeit with a generous assist from Fellows. Taylor salvaged third place.

In the separate GT race, the Porsche GT1 made a sucessful SportsCar debut in the hands of Dorsey Schroeder and Andy Pilgrim, besting Doc Bundy and Andy Wallace in the Panoz GTR-1, second overall and second in GTS-1.

Third overall were Franz Konrad and Nick Ham, winners of the GTS-2 category in a Porsche 911 GT2. Next in line at the finish was the remarkable BMW M3 of Javier Quiros and Derek Hill, followed by a sister M3 piloted by teammates Boris Said and Marc Duez. They dominated the GTS-3 class.

Exxon World SportsCar/
Exxon Supreme GT
Presented by Virgin Interactive
Championship Race 8
SportsCar Grand Prix
Las Vegas Motor Speedway
Las Vegas, NV
September 21, 1997
1.94 Mile Road Course

BUTCH LEITZINGER AND FORD WIN UNDER LIGHTS IN LAS VEGAS

Las Vegas is a nighttime city and, fittingly, the Las Vegas round of the Exxon World SportsCar series was scheduled for an 8:30 pm start. Two hours later, Butch Leitzinger, who had put his Dyson R&S Ford on the pole, was in victory circle along with co-driver John Paul Jr., still recovering from his Indianapolis crash injuries. Paul, who started the car, was immediately passed by Andrea Montermini in the Moretti Ferrari 333SP and teammate Elliott Forbes-Robinson in the other Dyson R&S Ford. By the time Leitzinger took over after 30 laps, his mount had been shuffled out of the top half dozen. However, the Moretti Ferrari suffered an overly long pit stop when Montermini came in for the drivers change to Antonio Hermann. Soon after the round of pit stops, James Weaver, Forbes-Robinson's teammate, was in the lead, with Leitzinger and Eric van de Poele in the R&S Olds in pursuit. When Weaver's engine quit, Leitzinger took over the point, then lost the lead to van de Poele on his pit stop. Leitzinger got the top spot back on lap 78 when van de Poele pitted. That effectively ended the contest with Leitzinger 12.230 seconds ahead of van de Poele at the finish. Late race heroics on the part of Montermini got back one lap of the two lap deficit he inherited from Hermann, and gained third place for the Ferrari.

In the separate GT race, Porsches prevailed in all three classes. Leader of the Porsche parade was the GT-1 of Allan McNish and Andy Pilgrim, first overall and first in class. GTS-2 fell to Price Cobb and Larry Schumacher who checked in sixth overall in their 911. David Murry and Jim Matthews took down GTS-3 honors in their 911, besting a strong BMW entry.

Exxon World SportsCar/
Exxon Supreme GT
Presented by Virgin Interactive
Championship Race 9
SportsCar Festival of Road Racing
Pikes Peak International Raceway
Fountain, CO
September 28, 1997
1.289 Mile Road Course

ANDREA MONTERMINI'S BIG COMEBACK PREVAILS AT PIKES PEAK

With six different leaders on its tight 1.29 mile road circuit, the SportsCar Festival at Pikes Peak was one of the more exciting outings in the Exxon World SportsCar series. While there were plenty of supporting players, the acknowledged star of the proceedings was Ferrari 333SP driver Andrea Montermini. First, he put the Moretti Ferrari on the pole. Electing to start, co-driver Antonio Hermann got outjumped immediately by John Paul Jr., in the Dyson R&S Ford, the first of a series of demotions which left the Moretti Ferrari almost two laps down when Montermini took over, 30 minutes into the race. In the next half hour, Montermini was up to fourth place and on the lead lap. By lap 86 he was in the lead, losing it only for six laps when he made his last pit stop. At the end, Montermini backed off to a 13.453 second margin of victory over second place Wayne Taylor in the R&S Olds. James Weaver, in the Dyson R&S Ford shared with Elliott Forbes-Robinson, finished third. Both he and fourth place teammates, John Paul Jr. and Butch Leitzinger, felt that they had widely missed the correct set up for the track.

In the separate GT event, Andy Pilgrim nailed down the year's GTS-1 title with his race winning effort in the Porsche GT1 shared with Allan McNish. Julian Bailey and Craig Baird in the Lister finished second overall, second in GTS-1. They put up a stiff fight, settled by pit stop time rather than on the track. Franz Konrad and Nick Ham were again the GTS-2 winners, clocking in at sixth overall. Bill Auberlen and Boris Said were the leaders of a three car BMW M3 train at the top of the GTS-3 standings. They were eighth overall.

Exxon World SportsCar/
Exxon Supreme GT
Presented by Virgin Interactive
Championship Race 10
NAPA Auto Sebring Octoberfest
Sebring International Raceway
Sebring, FL
October 18, 1997
3.718 Mile Road Course

MOMO FERRARIS FINISH 1-2 AT SEBRING WITH ANDREA MONTERMINI IN FRONT

Tires told the story at Sebring's two hour fall race, Dyson R&S Ford drivers James Weaver and Butch Leitzinger, out in front with the race half run, elected to stay with slicks when the rains came. They guessed wrong, had to pit under green to correct their mistake. The Momo Ferraris immediately and, correctly, as it turned out, switched to rain tires. Polesitter Andrea Montermini, rapidly making up the handicap handed to him by starting driver Antonio Hermann, made a daring pass on Didier Theys in the other Momo Ferrari in the wet and motored away for a 35.131 second winning margin at the checker. Theys, partnered by Freddy Lienhard, managed to hang on to the runner-up spot. Leitzinger made up for some of the tire error and salvaged third place. Weaver managed fifth place behind the Eliseo Salazar, Rob Morgan, Dean Hall Ferrari 333SP.

In the separate GT event, Eric Bernard, the polesitter, in the Panoz GTR-1 crossed the finish line first. However, the victory and GTS-1 honors went to the Andy Pilgrim-Allan McNish Porsche GT1 on the basis of a penalty assessed to Bernard for hitting McNish and spinning him on the last lap. Porsche mounted Larry Schumacher and Price Cobb finished fourth overall, first in GTS-2. Sixth overall and GTS-3 winners were BMW drivers Bill Auberlen and Marc Duez, clinching the division's manufacturer's championship for BMW.

Exxon World SportsCar/
Exxon Supreme GT
Presented by Virgin Interactive
Championship Race 11
VISA SportsCar Championship
Laguna Seca Raceway
Monterey, CA
October 26, 1997
2.238 Mile Road Course

BUTCH LEITZINGER TAKES THE WSC TITLE IN STYLE WITH LAGUNA SECA WIN

Butch Leitzinger didn't have to win the season finale at Laguna Seca to take the World SportsCar driver's championship. Although Rob Morgan had a mathematical chance, realistically, all Leitzinger had to do was beat his Dyson teammates, Elliott Forbes-Robinson and James Weaver who had the second and third best points totals going into the race. Win he did, however, with a little help from the racing gods. Eric van de Poele, in the R&S Olds, incurred a pair of penalties for overshooting the pits, Dyson teammate James Weaver and Ferrari driver Fermin Velez tangled, delaying them both, and polesitter Andrea Montermini's late charge in the Momo Ferrari fell short. This collection of others' mishaps let Leitzinger into the lead on lap 58. He ran out the race with a handy 21.725 second lead, to secure his first WSC title. Montermini's blast through the field gained him runner-up honors. Even with the penalties, van de Poele and co-driver Wayne Taylor managed third place. Weaver, ended up seventh, still good enough to earn co-driver Forbes-Robinson runner-up honors in the year's title chase and third place for himself.

The separate GT race turned out to be a Panoz benefit. With the arch rival Rohr Motorsports Porsche GT1 out due to a testing accident, Andy Wallace took the pole in his Panoz, while David Brabham, in the sister car, qualified alongside him on the front row. Wallace broke a brake rotor four laps from the end, handing victory to his teammate. GTS-2 again went to the Porsche pair of Franz Konrad and Nick Ham, who finished third overall. Dieter Quester and Marc Duez drove the top BMW M3 of the three that swept the GTS-3 category.

Geoffrey HHewitt

Donald Panoz's Ford-powered Panoz GTR-1 was a sensation on the GTS circuit.